SHAKSPERE FORGERIES

IN

THE REVELS ACCOUNTS

SHAKSPERE
FORGERIES

IN

THE REVELS ACCOUNTS

SAMUEL A. AARON TANNENBAUM, 1874? - 1948.

Time shall vnfold what plighted Cvnning-
(ham) hides   *Shakspere-Furness*

KENNIKAT PRESS, INC./PORT WASHINGTON, N. Y.

SHAKSPERE FORGERIES IN THE REVELS ACCOUNTS

To

ASHLEY HORACE THORNDIKE

IN PROFOUND GRATITUDE

PREFATORY NOTE

MODERN scientific methods have caused us not only to modify views previously held, but in some cases even to reverse those views in their entirety. Even in matters of such relatively slight importance as the biographic details in the "lives" of literary men, this turn about may be no less complete and often no less dramatic and difficult of acceptance. Convictions and beliefs which have been long held are not easily rejected. Notwithstanding the steadily increasing number of persons acquiring a university education and scientific training, the world is still largely "deaf to new music." To compel acceptance of the results of modern research, the proponent of a new view has a double task before him: he must disprove the view formerly held—in the course of which he must of necessity criticize those responsible for the erroneous view—and he must establish the truth of the view he has discovered. Unless he does both, it will rarely be considered that he has succeeded in his task.

That the matters dealt with by the investigator are not of great consequence does not make his task any easier. To millions of mankind the subject discussed in this book is of no importance whatsoever. Only an infinitesimal fraction of that small class of the reading public who do not feed exclusively on fiction and palatably seasoned science—"delicious poison"—will or can have the slightest interest in such a trivial question as whether certain presumably ancient accounts or bills are or are not genuine. Their interest will not be stirred even when they are informed that these accounts have been the subject of learned discussion and acrimonious debate during much of the past eighty-five years; that they purport to be the official accounts of two Masters of the Revels of the reign of King James I; that, if genuine, they give us information regarding Shakspere's popularity at Court up to and even after his supposed retirement from active connection with the London stage; that they witness to the esteem in which the royal family held certain of Shakspere's earliest plays, to wit, *The Comedy of Errors, Love's Labor's Lost*, and *The Merchant of Venice*; that they furnish us with data tending to establish the date of composition of such great plays as *Measure for Measure, Othello, The Tempest*, and *The Winter's Tale*.

To those who are not acquainted with the history of the growth of Shakspere's reputation, with the evolution of Shaksperian criticism, with the determination of the chronological order of the works of the greatest of England's poets,—to these this book will have not a particle of interest. But to the small group of serious students of the history of our literature, especially that chapter of it which deals with William Shakspere, the book must, I flatter myself, have considerable appeal. After all, Shakspere's is the greatest name in English literature, in all literature; and anything that contributes to our knowledge of him and his work, or purports to do so, must receive some attention and needs no apology for its existence.

But is this true of a book, such as this, which is devoted, not to adding to our store of data regarding the great dramatist, but to proving that certain data now generally accepted by scholars and incorporated in our books are based on spurious documents? Undoubtedly, yes. False data are worse than no data. Those who are acquainted with the manifold mischiefs wrought by the forgeries of that learned and unprincipled scholar, John Payne Collier, will have no doubt as to the value of running to earth any spurious document and eliminating it from future research.

Many will no doubt regret, as I do,

that as a result of the application of the technique of the modern science of bibliotics¹ to the suspected documents, the treasury of ascertained "facts" regarding Shakspere—those poor remains which must serve as the frail skeleton upon which we build the "life" of Shakspere—must become poorer by something like a dozen items. We shall have to continue ignorant regarding a revival of *The Comedy of Errors*, *The Merchant of Venice*, *The Merry Wives of Windsor*, and *Henry the Fifth* in the winter season of 1604-5; regarding the existence of *Measure for Measure* as early as December 26, 1604; regarding a performance of *Othello* in November, 1604; also regarding performances of *The Tempest* and of *The Winter's Tale* in the winter of 1611. But, fortunately, our understanding and appreciation and love of Shakspere will not suffer even the slightest diminution by the rejection of the data contained in the questioned Accounts. And even if they did so, our respect for historical truth would leave us no choice in the matter.

ACKNOWLEDGMENTS

IN discharging the pleasant duty of acknowledging my many obligations to my friends and acquaintances who have assisted me in one way or another in the preparation of this book, "I were best to call them generally, man by man, according to the scrip." Professor Joseph Quincy Adams, of Cornell University, read my manuscript twice, each time—as might have been expected—making valuable suggestions and propounding problems for me to solve and difficulties to meet. Dr. C. F. Ansley, of the Columbia University Press, edited my manuscript and read the proofs as conscientiously and painstakingly as if the book had been his own. My association with him has been one of the pleasantest by-products of this book. Mr. Max I. Baym, the author of *Symbols and I*, has given me the benefits of his scrupulous analysis of my whole thesis. To Mr. Frederick Coykendall, the Director of the Columbia University Press, I am indebted for the publication of the book, for his great interest in it, and for the beautiful format that he has given it. Professor Joseph Vincent Crowne, of the College of the City of New York, has read parts of the manuscript and made many excellent suggestions. Professor Albert Feuillerat, of the University of Rennes, and at present Exchange Professor at Columbia University, has patiently listened to part of my argument and most kindly examined and studied parts of the fabricated documents which I had found unintelligible and incomprehensible. With his wonted generosity, Dr. Horace H. Furness, Jr., has placed his Shaksperian treasures at my disposal and permitted me to reproduce Sir William Musgrave's letter to Edmund Malone. Dr. Alexander Green has unselfishly devoted much valuable time to editing the manuscript before it went to press as well as to proofreading and editing afterwards. Mr. Harris J. Griston, the author of the startling and intriguing *Shaking the Dust from Shakespeare*, has given me the benefit of his examination of part of my arguments. Professor Ernest H. C. Oliphant has borne—with many a patient shrug, methinks—the burden of listening to the successive steps in the evolution of my thesis. He has critically studied my photographs of the documents, my arguments, and the language in which I clothed them. Dr. Joseph Pearl, of the College of the City of New York, has been of great assistance to me in connection with the two paragraphs of dog Latin in one of the manuscripts. Dr. A. S. W. Rosenbach has not only permitted me to study and photograph Collier's three-volume manuscript of *Emendations and Notes to Old English Plays*, but has placed the whole of his invaluable collection of manuscripts and books at my disposal. What this means can be appreciated only by one engaged in research. Mrs. Charlotte Carmichael Stopes, the foremost Shaksperian scholar of her sex, has befriended me in more ways than can be told here. To Professor Ashley H. Thorndike I am indebted most. He had no sooner read my manuscript than, without being solicited thereto and without the slightest delay, he arranged to have the book published. It was he who gave me the opportunity to demonstrate my thesis before a distinguished audience in a lecture at Columbia University a little more than three years ago.

Others who have assisted me in one way or another are Miss Margaret Schlauch, of New York University, the author of a splendid work on *Chaucer's Constance and Accused Queens*; Mr. Frederic W. Erb, of Columbia University Library; the employees of the Columbia University Press; and the officials of the English Government Laboratories, of the Bodleian Library, of the Public Record Office, and of the Manuscript Department of the British Museum.

In expressing my many obligations to the staffs of the Columbia University Press and of the Strawberry Hill Press, I must single out Mr. Charles G. Proffitt and Mr. George Grady.

To all, my best thanks.

S. A. T.

New York.

CONTENTS

LIST OF FACSIMILES

CHAPTER ONE

INTRODUCTORY AND HISTORICAL

THE story of the forged "Revels Accounts of 1604-5 and 1611-12," also known as the "Cunningham papers," presents many points of interest to the literary historian, the psychologist, and the paleographer.[1] Though the mystery surrounding these papers will probably never be wholly solved, it will interest historians of the Elizabethan drama to know who concocted them, who wrote them, what motives prompted the forger, how they are related to other forgeries before and after them, what sources the forger had for some of the data incorporated in them, whether he worked from now lost originals, and why it is that recent investigators have not recognized the true character of these documents.

The history of the documents is a succession of blunders and mystifications. In 1842, Peter Cunningham, a young man of twenty-six, employed as a clerk in the Audit Office, in London, and known to be an enthusiastic and zealous member of the Shakespeare Society, announced his discovery, "in a dry and lofty cellar" at Somerset House, of two official books of Revels Accounts. One of these related to Edmund Tyllney's and the other to George Buc's administration of the office of Master of the Revels—the former covering the years

1604-5 and the latter the years 1611-12. This "find" caused quite a stir among Shaksperian scholars; for these papers apparently settled for all time the vexed questions of the dates of composition and production of *Measure for Measure*, *Othello*, *The Winter's Tale*, and *The Tempest*. Cunningham thereupon published,[2] under the auspices of the (old) Shakespeare Society, what everybody has supposed to be a faithful transcript of the documents in question, together with all prior Revels Accounts. It did not occur to anyone to doubt the genuineness of the newly discovered papers.

A quarter of a century later, in 1868, Cunningham, who meanwhile had become a victim of chronic alcoholism and had lost his position in the Civil Service, offered to sell to the British Museum the Books of Accounts he had discovered.[3] Sir Frederic Madden, then Keeper of Manuscripts in the Museum, thereupon took steps, successfully, to recover these papers as national property, not subject to sale by any private individual.

But the matter did not end there. Almost immediately after the documents had been deposited in the national archives, it was announced in the press that experts had examined the papers and declared parts of them—the most important parts of them—to be forged.

Coming shortly after the exposure of John Payne Collier's notorious and vexatious forgeries in the much discussed "Perkins Folio" and in certain alleged Elizabethan documents, the announcement that the two lists of plays, "in which were included many of Shakespeare's greatest works, with the dates of their being acted before King James at Whitehall, were entirely forged," naturally caused a great sensation. The old disputes about the dates of *Othello* and of other Shaksperian plays were reopened with the ardor characteristic of Shakspere enthusiasts, and Peter Cunningham, by then the author of *The Life of Inigo Jones* and *The Story of Nell Gwynne* and the editor of Horace Walpole's *Letters*, was generally condemned as a forger.

It should be mentioned at this point that "one or two experts and critics hinted pretty broadly that Cunningham was probably only the tool, jackal or dupe of Collier and that behind the pitiful figure of the broken-down drunkard lurked the sinister and ubiquitous hand of the arch-fabricator—the disgraced scholar, the treacherous friend, who, abusing the trust reposed in him and the unexampled opportunities and privileges accorded him, had prostituted his learning, his knowledge and skill, in the vile and mischievous work of poisoning the springs of research into the life and works of our supreme poet."[4]

Even this, however, failed to settle the matter. In 1880 Halliwell-Phillipps announced that while working in the Bodleian Library he had discovered among the "Malone papers"—a body of documents presented to that library in 1821, nine years after Edmund Malone's death—a sheet of paper which contained a list of Shakspere's plays, with the dates of their performance at Court in 1604-5, and which all but exactly tallied with Cunningham's list, even to certain eccentricities of spelling.

Exactly when this sheet of paper, now generally referred to as the "Malone scrap" or the "scrap," and known at the Bodleian as *Malone MS. No. 29, f. 69ᵛ*, was acquired by the library is not certain. No one knows whether it was among the "Malone papers" when these were purchased by the Bodleian, or whether it was subsequently added to the collection. It is not in Malone's handwriting; nor was it cited by James Boswell, who in 1821 published a revised edition of Malone's *Variorum Shakespeare*, incorporating data obtained from Malone's papers. There is, indeed, extant evidence to show that Malone had information concerning the dates of the earliest performances of *Othello* and *The Tempest* which tallied almost exactly with information contained in the Cunningham papers and was unknown to other scholars. But the source of his information is not known. It was therefore assumed by Halliwell-Phillipps that, inasmuch as he could not doubt the authenticity of the Malone "scrap," because it was found among Malone's papers, the suspected Revels Accounts must have been forged reproductions of all or part of genuine records that had been lost, hidden away, or destroyed. He took it for granted that the forger had discovered two genuine Books of Accounts, in both of which there happened to be some blank pages, of which he availed himself to introduce his fabricated data concerning some of the plays by Shakspere, Heywood, Chapman, Greene, and others.

All this only added to the mystery. The late Dr. Furness, after careful consideration, expressed the matter well in his edition of *The Tempest* in 1892. He then wrote: "The puzzle of these Revels Accounts may some day be solved. At present it is inscrutable." After that pronouncement the *play-lists* in these documents—and only they—were generally regarded as forgeries, but the information contained in them was accepted as, in the main, genuine.

There the matter rested until 1911, when the zealous and industrious Mr. Law, investigating the history of performances in Hampton Palace, came across these documents and decided to have them examined anew and tested by paleographic experts. Professor Charles W. Wallace, Sir Henry Maxwell-Lyte, Sir George Warner, and others scrutinized the documents carefully and declared, apparently without any hesitation, that they saw nothing spurious *or even suspicious* about them. They were unanimous in their verdict that the papers were what they purported to be.

To remove all possible doubt, it was decided to submit the papers to Professor Sir James J. Dobbie, an expert chemist at the head of the Government Laboratories, for his opinion as to the ink, inasmuch as it was the ink, more than anything else, that had caused Halliwell-Phillipps to pronounce against the genuineness of the papers. The examination was made, and Professor Dobbie reported, according to Mr. Law, that the suspected play-lists were genuine, and that the ink with which they were written presented no suspicious features and was identical with that in the other pages. This, it was thought, would at last settle the matter for all time.

But no sooner was Mr. Law's book published than the documents were severely attacked on paleographic as well as on historical grounds by Mrs. Charlotte C. Stopes, writing under the pseudonym "Audi Alteram Partem," in a series of letters published in the pages of *The Athenæum*. Mr. Law met every one of his opponent's historical objections so adroitly that it was generally acknowledged that he had completely vindicated the authenticity of the Cunningham documents and, with that, the character of the alleged forger.[5]

In 1922 Mrs. Stopes boldly reopened the controversy in a pamphlet entitled *The Seventeenth Century Accounts of the Masters of the Revels*, in which she maintained, very plausibly and cogently, that these documents contained many errors of a kind of which no real Clerk of the Revels could have been guilty.[6] Even this, however, did not put an end to the controversy. A new champion, my friend Mr. W. J. Lawrence, now entered the lists in behalf of his countryman, the much maligned Cunningham. In a clever little essay[7] he maintained that the errors committed by the "Clerk" were such as might be attributed to nothing more than a natural capacity for blundering. The discrepancies between the Accounts and the correlative warrants issued by the Treasurer of the Chamber, also published in 1842 by Cunningham,

Mr. Lawrence considered rather as evidence of the genuineness of the suspected papers. "A forger," said he, not unplausibly, "would surely have taken care that all the dates were in harmony, that there should be equivalence."

But the strongest argument—an unassailable one, apparently—in favor of the authenticity of the Cunningham papers advanced by Mr. Lawrence was this: the play-list of 1611-12 refers to an old play, *Hymen's Holiday*, in a manner which, he thinks, implies knowledge not available in 1842. His point is that some of the information embodied in the list involves a fact—William Rowley's connection with the Duke of York's Men —which was wholly unknown prior to 1849. Mrs. Stopes's reply to Mr. Lawrence gave the impression that the documents were really not so glaringly at fault in their contents as to warrant their rejection as forgeries. The matter of the ink and the penmanship, to which she had previously objected, had now ceased to be a subject for discussion, doubtless because of the weight of the opinions of Mr. Law's experts, and as to these matters she now was silent.

In January, 1925, the late Mr. D. T. B. Wood, of the British Museum, published a short but important paper[8] in which he maintained that the Malone "scrap" was in the handwriting of Sir William Musgrave, First Commissioner of the Board of Audit for part of the last decade of the eighteenth century. The significance of this will be realized when it is considered that Sir William had written to Malone, on November 7, 1791, that arrangements had been made for his (Malone's) inspection of certain documents at Somerset House, and that on December 2, 1799, he sent Malone "a Mem[dum] about a MS which you have probably met with already—if not it may furnish matter for some of your illustrations of Shakespear." The reader must not jump to the conclusion, however, that Musgrave, in his letter of 1791, had the Accounts of 1604-5 and of 1611-12 in mind. That he did *not* have them in mind is sufficiently evident from the fact that Malone, in 1796, ended his published account of the English stage with the statement that "There is no subsequent Revels Account [*i. e.*, subsequent to 1588] in the reign of Queen Elizabeth now extant." (Boswell, re-editing Malone in 1821, made no comment on this statement—clear proof that he had not seen the Malone "scrap" among the papers which had been entrusted to him and which subsequently became part of the Bodleian Library.) But there is no denying that Mr. Wood's article made a profound impression on scholars interested in the matter.

A few months later Mr. Wood showed[9] conclusively that the paper on which the Accounts were written was genuine paper of the period. This was really unnecessary, since no one had ever questioned the genuineness of the paper. And anyone connected with the British Museum, the Public Record Office, or Somerset House, would have had no difficulty in obtaining sheets of genuine paper manufactured in the Elizabethan and Jacobean periods. Almost all the twelve extant Books of the Revels in the reign of Elizabeth contained, and still contain, numerous blank pages and even blank sheets.[10]

In the light of the work done by Mr. Law, Mr. Lawrence, and Mr. Wood, scholars had no choice but to accept the Cunningham papers as paleographically genuine and their data as historically authentic. The late Sir Sidney Lee, for example, wrote: "The authenticity of the documents was completely vindicated by Mr. Ernest Law."[11] In his encyclopedic work, *The Elizabethan Stage*,[12] Sir Edmund K. Chambers, though acknowledging that "there are some singular things about the substance of the [Revels] books," thinks it is no longer possible, "in view of the paleographical investigation ... to reject the genuineness of the 1604-5 list." As to the 1611-12 list, he concedes that "the facts necessitate some caution" in their use. In what is perhaps one of the very latest published utterances on the subject,[13] Professor F. S. Boas expresses the conviction that Mr. Wood has rendered "an important service to scholarship by establishing beyond all reasonable doubt the genuineness of the Revels Books for 1604-5, and inferentially of those of 1611-12 and 1636."

In the ensuing pages I shall show that the inspection of the documents by the paleographers of the last decade was superficial and casual, not competent to determine anything scientifically; that the papers had not been studied by the method of the science of bibliotics; that the chemical examination of the ink was wholly inadequate to the issues involved; and that Mr. Law, and therefore his readers also, misinterpreted the chemist's report. At the same time I shall also show (1) that these Cunningham papers, with the exception of some eight or nine lines (see Appendix E), are forgeries from beginning to end; (2) that these papers present abundant evidence of tampering; (3) that the penmanship is not that of the Official Clerk of the Revels who is alleged to have written them; (4) that the writing is the studied work of one who was not accustomed to the Old English script which it imitates; (5) that the Malone "scrap" was not written by Sir William Musgrave; (6) that it is not the faithful transcript of the 1604-5 play-list which it is said to be; (7) that there is no evidence extant to show that it was in existence prior to 1868, the year in which Cunningham tried to dispose of his "papers"; (8) that it was in all probability a cleverly conceived "plant" introduced by the forger among Malone's papers for the purpose of bolstering up the claim of the suspected play-lists; (9) that the forger was, as some had thought, actually John Payne Collier; and (10) that his purpose in concocting these forgeries was mainly to corroborate some of his guesses about Shakspere and his contemporaries.

CHAPTER TWO

THE INK AND THE CHEMIST'S REPORT

BOTH Mr. Wood and Mr. Law based an important part, perhaps the most important part, of their case on the testimony of the late Professor Dobbie, the Principal of the Government Laboratories of England. Mr. Law long ago realized the vital importance of the question concerning the character of the ink with which the documents were written. In his first book on the subject (SSF, p. 66), in a discussion of page 3 of the Accounts for 1611-12, he wrote that "to the ordinary eye, even when assisted with a magnifying-glass, it [the ink] appears, in every point and particular, exactly like that on the other side of the leaf, as well as in the whole of the rest of the document ... Yet it was precisely the peculiarity in the character of the ink which was cited by Halliwell-Phillips [sic] as fatally discrediting the writings, and proving them both [i.e., the ink and the writings] to be of a period long subsequent to the seventeenth century... The modern 'character of its ink'! This, in fact, had been just the decisive point, which had weighed more than any of the confident asseverations of all the commentators and all the experts. If the ink was plainly and *unmistakably recent*, then the playlists were, of course, forgeries ... But if the 'character of the ink' was, on the contrary, anything but suspicious—in fact, *in all ways and in all appearances absolutely ancient and original*, what then?" (Italics mine here and in following quotations.)

Having obtained the opinions of Professor Charles W. Wallace and Sir George Warner that the documents were genuine, Mr. Law felt (*loc. cit.*, p. 69) that "there would have seemed something inconclusive about the whole thing, unless the *crucial and unanswerable* tests of microscopical and chemical analyses were applied to the papers and the ink ... If ... it [the ink] was shown to be ancient, the demonstration would be overwhelming and conclusive." The Books of Revels for 1604-5 and 1611-12 were accordingly, through the hearty co-operation of Sir Henry Maxwell-Lyte, Deputy Keeper of the Public Records, forthwith submitted to Professor Dobbie "for examination and testing." Some time thereafter "an elaborate report" of the laboratory findings was furnished to the Deputy Keeper. (For this report see Appendix A, pp. 63-64.)

"The conclusions of the Government Analyst," wrote Mr. Law (*loc. cit.*, p. 71), "are 'that *the ink used is of the same character throughout the document*,' and that 'there is no evidence to support the suggestion that the writing on pages 3 and 4 [the suspected list of plays] is of a different date from the writing on the remainder of the document.'"

Now let us see what Mr. Wood has to say on the subject of the ink, and how far he agrees with Mr. Law and with Professor Dobbie. After establishing the genuineness of *the paper* on which these Accounts are written, Mr. Wood says: "It is fair to point out that curious and apparently *unnecessary alterations and erasures* occur *in a different ink* from that of the [play-]lists, and that these [alterations and erasures] occur only in the lists and not in the accounts.' The ink as a whole has faded dark grey, but the ink of the corrections and erasures has faded light brown ... The worst point against the ink is what I have called the 'woolly' appearance of the 1604-5 list—it gives very much the idea of ink blotted with blotting-paper and not sanded.² I am told that under the microscope it reveals itself to be laid on quite thick, like paint, and cracked in the same way." This, it will be conceded, is not only very unlike Mr. Law's account of the matter, but possibly of the utmost importance in the subject we are now investigating.

It may naturally be asked, why did not Mr. Wood take steps to have the ink and the writing re-examined if he realized that his observations did not agree with those of Mr. Law? The answer obviously is that he relied on Professor Dobbie's report as Mr. Law cited it, for he says (*loc. cit.*): "The chemical composition of the ink has been tested at the National Laboratory and [has been] adjudged to be all of the same date and all ancient. If we accept

this, 'cadit quaestio,' no modern forgery is possible."

It all narrows down, then, to the chemist's report on the ink. If Professor Dobbie had said what Mr. Law and Mr. Wood credit him with having said—neither of them quotes his words!—and if Professor Dobbie had been an expert chemist and had made a scientific and thorough investigation of the matter, there would be an end to the question.

But, as a matter of fact—and I say this after long and careful deliberation—Professor Dobbie did *not* report what has been attributed to him. What he really reported, as we learn from Mr. Law himself (*op. cit.*, pp. 70-71) and from an official transcript of part of the chemist's report, now preserved in the Public Record Office at London, was this:

"When examined microscopically, the ink presents similar characteristics throughout the whole document ... No difference is discernible ... between the ink on pages 3 and 4, and that in other parts of the document ... The chemical examination gave no indication of any difference, either in the constituents of the ink or in the degree of resistance to bleaching agents, between the ink on pages 3 and 4, and that in other portions of the document examined.

"A consideration of all the observations made in the course of the examination shows that *the ink used is of the same character throughout* the document. [Mr. Wood, I may remind the reader, does not agree with Professor Dobbie as to this.]

"There is no evidence in my opinion to support the suggestion that the writing on pages 3 and 4 is of a different date from the writing on the remainder of the document."

The reader will note that in the above report there is not a word said about the ink's being "absolutely ancient and original"! Professor Dobbie nowhere described the ink as "ancient." As a matter of fact, he was very careful to say merely that the ink on pages 3 and 4 does not differ from that in other parts of the document, except as to all but one of the signatures. *He does not say that the ink is ancient; he does not say that the writing is ancient or genuine.*

But in fairness to the memory of Sir James, it must be said that the special task which had been assigned him was not to determine *the age* of the ink but rather "to ascertain whether there was evidence that the ink on pages 3 and 4 [in an 'Account Booke of Revels' written in the year 1605] is of different character or of different age from the ink in other portions of the document."[3] (Quoted from a letter written me by Mr. George Stubbs, Deputy Government Chemist, from the English Government Laboratory, June 19, 1924, and subsequently confirmed by an exact transcript of Professor Dobbie's report.)

It follows, then, that though Mr. Law fully appreciated the value of "crucial and unanswerable tests of microscopical and chemical analyses applied to the papers and the ink," no such examinations were really made. There is nothing in Professor Dobbie's report to show that *the paper* was examined, either chemically or microscopically. Surely the tests applied to the "ink" in ten spots on pages 2, 3, and 4 (only!) cannot

be characterized as "unanswerable;" Professor Dobbie had not been asked to determine *the age* of the "ink." Professor Dobbie, unlike Mr. Law, was very careful to refrain from saying anything which might be construed as signifying that he considered *any part* of the 1604-5 document, the only one he examined, unquestionably genuine.

Neither is there in Professor Dobbie's report the slightest warrant for Mr. Law's assertion that "it has been *demonstrated* ... that the ink is *not modern* at all—neither in appearance, nor in mechanical effect, nor in chemical constitution." Professor Dobbie said not a word about the age of the "ink" and made no such demonstration.

Mr. Law is unquestionably right when he says that if it were shown that the ink was "ancient, the demonstration [of the genuineness of the questioned documents] would be overwhelming and conclusive." But, we must repeat, Professor Dobbie said not a single syllable about the ink's being *ancient*. He knew, I take it, even though Mr. Law evidently does not, that there are no chemical or microscopical tests whereby one may prove "overwhelmingly and conclusively" that certain ink marks are "ancient." If Professor Dobbie had assumed—as he seems to have done—that the other pages of the Accounts for 1604-5 which had been submitted to him are genuine and ancient, he could properly have argued only that if these pages are genuine, and if the ink is the same throughout the document, then are pages 2 and 3 also genuine.

Mr. Law is guilty of another over-statement when he says that Professor

Dobbie "made a technical and scientific examination of *the writings* in question." The only possible basis for Mr. Law's assertion is the following passage—not quoted or reported by him—in the chemist's report: "There are several alterations on pages 3 and 4; '1605' at the head of page 3 has been altered to '1604'; the word 'Names' in the margin of page 3 has been crossed out with transverse lines; the letter 'e' has been added to the words 'on' and 'Spanisch' [should be 'Spainshe'] on page 4; and the letters 'ye' have been written over the final letter 'e' of 'tragide' on page 4. The ink used in making these alterations does not appear to be different in character from that on the other pages."[4] But this certainly does not constitute "a technical and scientific examination of the writings." His report shows that he omitted to examine *chemically* the "alterations" as well as the original versions of the altered words in the play-lists.

That Professor Dobbie, expert chemist though he was, would have been at best wholly unqualified for the task of making a technical examination of the writing, is indubitably shown by his failure to see—an omission of which Mr. Wood, too, was guilty—that the word "Tragidye" (*cf.* facsimile 3) *underlies* the word "Tragide" and that the italic *e*'s in the words "one" and "Spainshe" are survivals of, not additions to, original outlines which were to be inked later. Had he been an experienced examiner of questioned documents he would have known that such "alterations" are not characteristic of genuine handwritings, and he would undoubtedly have submitted the ink of the underlying and partially erased letters to a careful chemical and microscopic examination. His failure to examine the chemical constitution of the ink of the added *e*'s and of the *ye* and of other suspicious-looking spots deprives his report of any value whatsoever, especially in the light of Mr. Wood's statement that the alterations are in a different ink. That Sir James did his work in a superficial and perfunctory manner is sufficiently attested by the fact that though he noticed the alterations, which are obvious even to the naked eye, he did not trouble to examine them chemically.

The ink, says Mr. Law, apparently on the authority of one of England's most expert chemists, has been *demonstrated not to be modern* in "chemical constitution." It will, no doubt, amaze scholars to be informed that there is not the slightest warrant for Mr. Law's assertion. Professor Dobbie said not a word about the chemical ingredients constituting the ink! But Mr. Law's assertion implies that inks of the Jacobean era had a peculiar chemical composition which can be distinguished from that of modern inks; also that Professor Dobbie made a differential examination. Professor Dobbie attempted no such differential examination.

"Absolutely ancient," says Mr. Law regarding the ink! Unless ink of the Jacobean era had a chemical composition or physical properties which positively differentiated it from modern ink and which could not be imitated by a forger, it would be impossible for anyone to prove the ink of such a questioned document to be "absolutely ancient." Professor Dobbie made no such claim.

To establish the ancient character of the ink, Professor Dobbie would have had to show (1) that in chemical composition the ink was the same as in specimens appearing in *unquestioned* documents of the period; (2) that in physical properties—color, penetration, fissuring, etc.—it tallied exactly with specimens in unquestioned documents; and (3) that it would have been impossible for a forger in the first half of the nineteenth century to manufacture such ink. But Professor Dobbie made no examination which would warrant such conclusions—though this is what he should have done—and made no statements which would warrant anyone in saying that he had. Mr. Law errs in saying that the examination of the ink and the writing "was of a most stringent and exhaustive character."

The foregoing criticism of Professor Dobbie's examination and of Mr. Law's distortion of the former's report does not, of course, prove the questioned documents to be forgeries. But it does prove that Professor Dobbie's examination was practically worthless, because it was superficially conducted and was utterly inadequate to settling any of the questions at issue. His examination and report have therefore left the matter exactly where it was when Halliwell-Phillipps, one of the most skilled archivists and conscientious scholars in the realm of letters in the last century, and his associates and confrères—Alexander Dyce, Richard Grant White, Duffus-Hardy, and others—declared the documents palpably gross forgeries. The only advance that has been made since then is embodied in Mr. D. T. Wood's statement that *the ink of the play-lists has a suspicious woolly appearance and cracks off like paint*. If Mr. Wood's statement is right—and my study of photographic enlargements of the writing long ago led me to the same conclusion[5]—we have proof here that the "ink" was not really ink, but an artificial concoction made to simulate ink, probably consisting of ink and some dye, with or without the addition of lampblack; that it was not "absolutely ancient and original"; and that the documents *are* forgeries.

In defense of the documents the point has been made, in personal correspondence, that Professor Dobbie evidently saw nothing suspicious about them—a circumstance which would seem to confirm their ancient and genuine nature. Whatever value this argument may have is more than offset, I think, by the following considerations: (1) The preceding analysis of Professor Dobbie's report leaves no doubt that he was wholly untrained for the task of examining questioned documents; (2) some of the most expert archivists of the middle of the nineteenth century had at a glance rejected the play-lists as forgeries.

CHAPTER THREE

CONCERNING THE SCRIVENER

WITHIN a very short time after the Trustees of the British Museum had obtained possession of the Revels Accounts which Peter Cunningham had offered to sell them, for a price to be fixed by J. P. Collier, the press took up the matter and made the shocking announcement that the newly recovered papers had fallen under the grave suspicion of having been tampered with. It was asserted that competent judges, experts, had arrived at the conclusion that the only pages of any importance in these Accounts—viz., the so-called "play-lists," "in which were included many of Shakespeare's greatest works, with the dates of their being acted before King James at Whitehall"—were recent forgeries. How thorough an examination of the impugned documents the alleged experts made, we have no means of knowing. The general opinion concerning the recovered pages is probably accurately expressed in the following quotation from an essay on "Literary Forgeries" published in *The British Quarterly Review*, January, 1869: "It only required a glance of the experts to discover that the list of Shakespeare's plays ... had been appended to the old documents by a modern hand. The trifling and uninteresting items of expenditure [incurred in the preparations for the performances of those plays] are genuine."

Mr. Law, accepting the opinion of the experts of the sixties that *the handwriting of the 1604-5 play-list differs from that in the rest of the documents*, attempts (SSF, p. 36) to meet the implication of forgery by the very simple and plausible suggestion that "the differences in the writing could easily have been accounted for on the obvious supposition that the two pages on which the 1604-5 play-list is written had been reserved [*i.e.*, left blank] on purpose by the Clerk of the Revels in order that the list of plays might be afterwards inserted, possibly by another hand."[1] In support of this conjecture Mr. Wood has recently pointed out that though the Clerk of the Revels was technically responsible for writing the Accounts, he need not himself have written them, although he signed them. Sir Edward Maunde Thompson is of the opinion[2] that the 1604-5 play-list was written "by a professional scribe, probably the Engrossing Clerk of the Revels Office."

But, as a matter of fact, *the play-list in Book A is in the same handwriting as the rest of that book.*[3] This is proved by the identity in the forms of the letters, their shading, their proportions, their spacing, their slant, the speed and the pen pressure with which the two writings were done. Facsimile no. 1 brings this home to the eye and the mind in a most convincing way. Mr. Law's statement (*op. cit.*, p. 57) that the scribe of the 1604-5 play-list "made use of a style of lettering different to that employed in the undoubtedly authentic portions of the documents"[4] is incorrect, and consequently his argument that the difference in the two hands proves the genuineness of the documents falls to the ground.

Concerning the identity of the penman or penmen of Book A, and presumably also of Book B, only Mr. Law seems to have made a definite statement. On page 64 of his first book he says that the skilled, "neat, clear, uniform and precise" penmanship of the documents, other than the questioned playlists, is "doubtless" [!] the handwriting of William Honyng, the Clerk of the Revels.[5] It would not be safe to infer from Mr. Law's use of the word "doubtless" that the experts he consulted agreed with him in his identification of William Honyng as the penman of all but the condemned pages. Concerning the identity of the latter he tells us only that the clerk wrote "a large, coarse and not very sure or uniform hand," and that, judged by his orthography, his use of the Jacobean vulgarism "aleven,"[6] his spelling the poet's name "Shaxberd," etc., he was an illiterate scribe.[7] That the Revels Office would have employed an illiterate scribe and would have had him engross the required list of plays are to me such unbelievable propositions that I prefer to think that in his many "blunders" and his "vulgarisms" we have indications of the mock antique of a forger.

If Mr. Law could have proved that the penmanship of the major portions of these books or pamphlets was really that of William Honyng, it would, of course, have gone a very great way toward establishing the genuineness of the suspected pages. But it is almost impossible that any clerk, and certainly such an experienced clerk as Honyng, would have left two blank pages in a Book of Accounts where they would just serve the purpose of a nineteenth-century forger. And while some of those who have recently examined these Books assert that pages 3 A and 4 A are not an interpolated sheet[8] but constitute the left half of the sheet of paper of which pages 9 and 10 constitute the right half, we must remember that Mr. Law is willing to assume that these pages were left blank by Honyng so as to enable someone to insert the list of plays presented before the royal family during the winter holidays of 1604-5. In support of his conjecture Mr. Law points out that "in a previous account-book" [viz., for the year 1587-88] there is a marginal note admonishing the clerk that "the names of the plays wold[9] be expressed." But to me the effect of this argument is more than counterbalanced by two considerations: (1) No list of plays accompanies the Accounts of 1587-89 [!], even though these Accounts contain no less than three blank folio leaves; (2) blank pages occur in almost every one of the extant early Revels Accounts.[10]

Mr. Law's confident identification of Honyng as the penman of the hitherto unquestioned portions of these documents was perhaps determined by a certain superficial resemblance between the writing in the Accounts under discussion and the acknowledged writing of Honyng—as this appears in A.O.15/1: "A warrante for Mr Preston to Haue xx^{li} yerely"[11]—as well as by the occurrence of certain similarities between what purport to be Honyng signatures on 8A and 7B—note especially the H's, the g's and the flourishes over the n's in certain words—and the name "Honyng" in other parts of the suspected documents. It must also be acknowledged that to casual or superficial observation the penmanship of these Accounts bears some resemblance to the unquestioned Accounts of 1587-89. But a careful study of the handwriting should convince one, readily enough, that (1) the play-lists and the bulk of the documents were written by one and the same penman, and (2) that that penman was neither William Honyng nor the clerk who wrote the Revels Accounts of 1587-89.[12]

Obviously, it would be too much to ask any reader to believe that both in 1605 and in 1612, and only then, the Clerk of the Revels deliberately left the names of the plays and the players to be added by the very same "illiterate scribe."[13] We are not surprised, therefore, to find Mr. Law asserting (op. cit., pp. 65-66) that "the handwriting [of the later play-list] differs very little, if at all, from that in the rest of the account-book . . . The bulk of it is in Gothic[14] character, with an intermixture of Italian script . . . but in no other respect is the writing different from that on the other side of the leaf —page 4—on which begins Sir George Buc's account for the year ending October 31, 1612." But it may be said, without the slightest fear of contra-

diction on the part of anyone capable of using his eyes, that *the penmanship of the two play-lists is identical.* No one can possibly have any doubt as to this if he will examine, in our facsimile 1b, corresponding letters and words in these two Books of Accounts, *e. g.*, the words "of," "Night," "the," "By," "Kings," "Play," and "Called," and the capital letters E, P, C, T, H, A, M, $\mathcal{Q}$, etc.

Taking as our "standard of comparison" Honyng's warrant (*cf.* facsimile 5) from Queen Elizabeth to pay Thomas Preston an annual pension of £20, we find that it differs from the writing in the impugned documents in so many respects that the supposition of their having been written by him becomes an impossibility. From a comparison of facsimiles 2, 3, and 5 it is easily apparent that Honyng's penmanship is sharply defined, fairly rapid and clear-cut, precise; whereas that of the writer of the Accounts—whom I shall designate as F—is vague, hesitant, slow, blurry. Certain varieties of letters, *e. g.*, the left-shouldered r, the open Old English a, the square-headed p, which are common in F, do not occur in Honyng. Other points of difference, *e.g.*, in the P, B, C, T, S, ll, and final f, will easily be discovered by one who takes the trouble to seek them out, but those I have pointed out are sufficient to prove that the writer of the Preston warrant, signed "Honynges"—variant for "Honynge"— did not write the suspected play-lists nor the remainder of the 1604-5 and 1611-12 Revels Accounts.

It is not unreasonable to suppose that Mr. Law thought the suspected Accounts were written by Honyng because he took it for granted that the Books of Accounts for 1587-89 were, as a matter of course, written by Honyng, who was then Clerk of the Revels, and that the handwriting is the same in all these Books of Accounts. To one not accustomed to the comparative study of handwritings, these two sets of writings —the Accounts for 1587-88, 1587-89, and those for 1604-5, 1611-12—look very much alike; but careful study shows that the latter, the suspected documents, are only a fairly good imitation, with a few slight intentional variations, of the penmanship of the earlier Accounts. The very striking differences between them are exhibited in facsimile 1c.

It will be noted that the forms or patterns of the letters, with the exception of the Old English *a*, the ampersand, the left-shouldered *r*, and the Old English final *f*, are the same in both, but that the writings differ in those more essential details which give individuality and character to a particular hand, and which therefore cannot be successfully imitated. These essential or personal characteristics are: shading, pen pressure, movement, speed, rhythm, alignment, slant, spacing, proportions, punctuation, and so forth.[15]

The preceding discussion has undoubtedly given the impression that Books A and B are, or seem to be, from beginning to end, in the same handwriting. But, as a matter of fact, they are not. Some eight or nine lines, and no more, are undoubtedly in another hand, a hand which I have been able to identify as that of the man whom I consider to have been the Engrossing Clerk, whoever he may have been. This hand is,

almost beyond doubt, the same hand that wrote the right half of *MS. Lansdowne 83, fo. 171*, transcribed in Professor Feuillerat's book, previously cited, at p. 418 (see facsimiles 4*b*, 7, and 8). That Halliwell-Phillipps, Alexander Dyce, Duffus-Hardy, Frederic Madden, Sir George Warner, Professor Wallace, Sir Henry Maxwell-Lyte, Professor Dobbie, Mr. Law, Mrs. Stopes, Mr. Wood, and others should have overlooked these bits written by this clerk, and failed to apprehend their significance, is one of the most amazing phenomena in this whole business. For, by a strange trick of fate, it so happens that these few bits, one in Book A and four in Book B, prove that *parts of these books are almost certainly genuine*. These fragments are as follows:

1. On page 9A, beneath what appears to be the signature "Ed Tyllney," there are these three lines, written in a beautiful hand and signed "Tho: fflemyng":

xix^{no} Decembris 1605
Edmundus Tylney Ar Magister de lez Revelles prestitit sacrum dc'is [=dictis] die et anno coram me.[16]

2. On the front cover of the 1611-12 Book, *i.e.*, on page 1B, the same hand wrote:

A^o x^{mo} Ris Jacobi.

3. On the back of the front cover, towards the bottom of page 2B, the clerk wrote this:

Receaved oute of his ma^{tis} Receipte at
westm' by privie Seale—CCiiij xiij^{li} xiiij^s iiij^d [17]

4. At the very bottom of 7B, just beneath the ostensible signatures of

G. Buc, A. Stafford, W^m: Honyng, and Edward kirkham, this clerk wrote:

Pred^t [=Predictus] Georgius Buc miles prestit sacruñ xvj^to Die Novembr. 1612 Anno D[ecimo] R[is] Jacobi.

This is signed "Jo: Sotherton: /:/." About two and a half inches above this, the same clerk wrote the figures "CClxxix^li xix^s" (*i.e.*, £279, 19s.), which he crossed out, then writing "CCiiij^li vij^s" (*i. e.*, £280, 7s.). Neither of these amounts, it may be noted now, tallies with the amount specified in item 3, above. And it must also be noted that the bits of writing by the Engrossing Clerk occur only on the first and last leaves of the suspected Revels Books.

The preceding considerations do not, of course, prove either Books A and B or the play-lists contained in them to be forgeries, unless one is convinced that the penmanship in those documents is an imitation of the penmanship of the 1587-89 Accounts. It is, to be sure, impossible to believe that in anything so unimportant as an annual itemized account of expenses incurred in dramatic entertainments, a public official would go to the trouble of imitating the penmanship of previous Accounts written by some other clerk. But whether the bulk of these documents is or is not such an imitation must be a matter of opinion; it cannot be proved. What I have proved is this: that the statements made by previous investigators of the subject are incorrect and valueless; that the documents are the work of at least two penmen; and that what appear to be remnants of the original Books of Accounts for 1604-5 and 1611-12 survive in the Books as we now have them.

FACSIMILE I.

a. IDENTITIES BETWEEN PLAY-LIST A AND BOOK A   *b*. IDENTITIES BETWEEN PLAY-LISTS A AND B

c. DIFFERENCES BETWEEN PLAY-LISTS A AND B AND THE ACCOUNTS OF 1587

Chapter Four

EXTERNAL CONSIDERATIONS

IN the course of his argument, Mr. Law, anticipating or meeting the objections of those who refuse to believe in the genuineness of the play-lists which give interest and value to these documents, makes several points which may perhaps be dealt with best in a chapter bearing the above general heading. At the same time I shall discuss certain matters which have not been considered either by him or by others, but which, none the less, are of great importance in connection with our inquiry.

1. Play-list A mentions the poet "Shaxberd" four times by name, twice in connection with a performance of *The Merchant of Venice*, once in connection with a performance of *Measure for Measure*, and once in connection with "The plaie of: Errors," presumably *The Comedy of Errors*. Those who had grown accustomed to the martial sound of the poet's surname could not bring themselves to accept as a legitimate variant a spelling which made of him a loquacious or waggish beard-shaker. The records of the doings of William Shakspere, his ancestors, and his posterity show between fifty and sixty ways of spelling the beloved bard's name, but in not even one is he called "Shaxberd." "Almost exactly similar peculiarities in the spelling of the immortal name

—*Shaxpere, Shaxber, Shaxbeer*—[are] plain indications, by the way, of the original universal pronunciation of the name," says Mr. Law (SSF, p. 57). But this is a very misleading statement of the facts. In over eight hundred occurrences of the poet's surname from 1550 to 1630, "Shaxber" is found only once and "Shaxbeer" twice; not once was the name spelled with a final *d*. The beard-shaking form of the name is, therefore, unique and peculiar to these Revels Accounts. To affirm that "the original universal pronunciation of the name" contained a *b* sound would be an assertion which could not be sustained by reference to only three instances in which the name was spelled authentically with a *b* in the second syllable. If Mr. Law means to imply that such spellings of the name as those he cites indicate that the poet's name was pronounced *shacks* (rhyming with *Jacks*) *ber* (or *per*), he evidently ignores the fact that in the English tongue the spelling of proper names—*e. g.*, Cholmondely, Blackstone, Southampton, Wriothesly, Wemyss, Burghley, Gloucester, and Alnwick—is not a dependable guide to their pronunciation.[1]

Sir Edward Thompson (*loc. cit.*) tried to defend the spelling "Shaxberd" on the theory that in the original draft, from which the Engrossing Clerk worked, Shakspere's name appeared as "*Shaxbere,* one of the recognized ways of spelling the name," and that the clerk mistook a final Old English "secretary" *e* for a *d.* This is ingenious but not convincing. "Shaxbere" was *not* one of the recognized ways of spelling the name; it occurs not even once in all the known records pertaining to the poet or to his family. And, furthermore, I cannot accept the view that a clerk in the Revels Office in 1605 could have been so ignorant as not to know the surname of the leading playwright and one of the most important actors of His Majesty's Players. To me "Shaxberd" sounds like the conceit of an ingenious modern fabricator, a man with the learning and the ingenuity of a Collier.

2. The "peculiar spelling" of these documents has been regarded as one of their suspicious features. And rightly so. Elizabethan penmen did not spell uniformly; they sometimes spelled even the simplest words differently within the limit of a single line. But did they ever spell so capriciously and so diversely as did the writer of the Accounts in question? The writer of the Revels Accounts of 1587 spelled much more uniformly. Thus the forger treats us to "Called," "Caled," and "Cauled"; "Moure" and "Moor" (altered from "Morr"); "play," "playe," and "plaie"; "wear" and "woere" (for "were"); "yere," "year," and "yeare"; "Bancketing," "Bancketting" and "Banketing"; "doson," "dousō," and "dosoun" (for "dozen"); "gett," "gaitt," and "geyt"; "night" and "nyght," etc. In all this there seems to be an obvious seeking for novelty and variety. The

forger was more Elizabethan than the Elizabethans.

3. The punctuation of the suspected play-lists has also been regarded as a suspicious phenomenon. The superabundance of colons in all sorts of places in which no punctuation marks are required is a striking feature in these papers. In his defense of the Accounts Mr. Law says, on page 17 of his *More about Forgeries* [MASF]: "The use of the colon is quite in accord with what is customary in other portions of the records of Revels." It will perhaps no longer astonish students to be informed that this statement is utterly incorrect. Nowhere in the Revels Accounts between 1571, the earliest extant, and 1589, the last prior to these of 1605, are colons used in the manner characteristic of the forged play-lists and Accounts. In the latter the colon is used as an ornamental [?] device (*e.g.,* "On the : 7 : of January was played/ the play of Henry the fift:"—"Hallamas Day being the first of : / Nouembar A Play in the Banketinge : / house") and not as a punctuation mark. Nothing like this, except rarely before and after numerals, occurs in the genuine Accounts. The "punctuation" in the 1612 Accounts is even more freakish than in those of 1605. In none of the genuine Accounts do we find anything like this: "The, names, of"—"Hallomas; Nyght" —"The: 5th of, nouember:"—"The, Sunday, ffollowinge."

Inasmuch as even an insane person has reasons for what he does—and I have not the slightest hesitation in saying that the perpetrator of these forgeries was a victim of monomania—it would be interesting to know why superfluous commas were introduced into the Book for 1611-12, and not into that for 1604-5. The only explanation that occurs to me is that the forger, or his accomplice, occasionally erred in the use of commas and therefore decided to cover up the error by a liberal sprinkling of commas throughout. Note, for example, that the scribe betrays great uncertainty about the performance of *The Silver Age*. He first tells us that on Sunday, January 12, there was a performance of "The Siluer Aiedg" and he puts a colon after "Aiedg"; then he adds the words "and ye next night following" and puts a period after "following"; but he evidently had his doubts whether anyone would believe that *The Silver Age*, or any other play, would have been produced before the Queen on two successive nights. He therefore ignores the period after "following" and adds the word "Lucrec," presumably Heywood's *The Rape of Lucrece*. That the word "Lucrec" was an after-addition is proved by the fact that it was squeezed into the line (the letter *e*—or, rather, what should be an *e*, but is not one—was added as an interlineation), is incomplete, was written with a different pen and at a different slant, and has a different alignment. (*Cf.* facsimile 6.)

Assuming that a forger would not invite scrutiny and suspicion by the introduction of novelties into his handiwork, one might ask: "Does not such a noticeable departure from precedent constitute evidence of genuineness?" But, strange as it may at first seem, the truth is that forgers often do absurd things. Thus, for example, a forger has been known to employ paper bearing a water-

mark subsequent to the date of the document. In one of his fraudulent concoctions John P. Collier employed paper with gilt edges in a document purporting to emanate from a time when gilt-edged paper was unknown.

4. In the opinion of some scholars acquainted with the Revels Accounts, *e.g.*, Professor E. H. C. Oliphant and the late Dr. Horace H. Furness, the presence of a column for the names of "The poets wch mayd the plaies" is a very suspicious feature in the 1605 play-list. Not a single one of the unquestioned Accounts, notably those of 1571, 1573, 1576, 1578, 1580, 1581, 1582, and 1584 —the only ones giving lists of plays— records the name of the author of a single play produced by the Master of the Revels. The name of the playwright was immaterial to the auditor of such accounts. Inasmuch as the names of the plays—*Measure for Measure*, etc.—were sufficient to identify the author for us, it is a fair inference that some of the poets were designated in the play-list of 1604-5 only for the purpose of introducing the variant "Shaxberd" to the literary world. And when one recalls that in 1839 and 1840 a lively battle of words was being fought in the pages of *The Gentleman's Magazine* concerning the orthography of the name of England's national bard, the contestants having been the Reverend Joseph Hunter, Sir Frederic Madden, Mr. John Bruce, Mr. Disraeli, Mr. Thomas Rodd, and others, it is almost impossible to avoid the inference that this quarrel in some way inspired the coinage "Shaxberd." Collier, I may add, was referred to in the discussion in a manner which

indicates that he was known to have been interested in the subject.

5. Those acquainted with the history of the famous "Perkins Folio" know that Collier's knowledge of Elizabethan English, extensive though it was, occasionally failed him and contributed to his exposure. In the Revels Accounts of 1611-12 there is one entry which, *me judice*, is worded in a manner that would have been impossible for an Elizabethan. The entry I have in mind reads: "On the : 24^ty: day of marche Being the Kings Ma^tis day/ of his Entrie to the Croune of England was performed at ye Tilt A Triumphe." 'The King's Majesty's day of his entry' is improbable, but "Entrie to the Croune" is well-nigh impossible, to say nothing of the "24^ty."

6. The dates in these documents present several suspicious features. Even Sir Edmund Chambers, who accepts the Accounts as genuine, "in view of the paleographical investigation," points out[2] that "the scribe has been oddly confused about his dates. On f. 1^v [*i.e.*, page 2A] he has written 'iij^o,' instead of 'ij^o,' for the regnal year. And at the top of f. 2 [*i.e.*, page 3A] he has apparently written '1605' and then corrected it to '1604.'"

To me it appears quite certain, from an examination of a photographic enlargement of page 3A, that the date was "1604" and was changed, in much darker ink, to "1605." The "5"—a very badly constructed and dilapidated figure —is larger than the "4" and almost hides it from view. There was no need for the scribe's alteration. Some of the earlier Revels Accounts bear on the first page the date of the year in which the Accounts begin, instead of that in which

they close, even though the rule is the other way. The point being of no consequence, a genuine clerk would not have given it a thought and would not have altered it. Mr. Law nowhere says anything about this tampered date, and by reproducing it as "160$\frac{5}{4}$" gives the erroneous impression that the scribe so wrote it, though such a dating would have been impossible then.

James ascended the English throne on March 24, 1603. The 31st day of October, 1604, from which day the 1604-5 Accounts profess to run, was therefore in the second year of the reign of King James; and yet a presumably competent clerk—William Honyng, according to Mr. Law—wrote (on page 2A): "the last of Octobar 1604: An^o RR^s Jacobi iij^o:"! The "clerk's" error is the more remarkable and the more significant when it is considered that in the paragraph immediately following the one containing this error—a paragraph which Cunningham failed to publish or even to mention!—the regnal year is correctly stated to be the second ("S$\tilde{c}$do").[3]

7. In connection with the error in the regnal date, it is, in all probability, of some significance that seven years later the same "clerk" experienced some difficulty in the matter of the regnal year when "transcribing" the accounts of 1611-12. On page 2B, in the opening paragraph, he left a space for the regnal year—an inconceivable omission with a real clerk, and almost impossible for William Honyng—which was subsequently inserted in different ink and, the space being too limited, in a smaller hand.

But this matter of the regnal date on page 2B possesses even greater interest than the preceding paragraph implies. On the front cover of Book B—*i.e.*, on page 1 B—3¾ inches from the top of the page, and the same distance from the right margin, there occurs this significant notation in the hand of the Engrossing Clerk (and, as it would seem, genuine): "A° x^mo R*is* Jacobi." This notation was not printed by Cunningham!—because he thought it contradicted the date on 2 B. We are therefore compelled to assume that the forger discovered parts of a genuine Book of Accounts for 1611-12, some of whose pages had been left blank, and that he used some of these pages in the manufacture of his Book for the year in question, but forgot, or thought it unnecessary, to erase the date on the front cover.

8. In the preface to his second book on these Accounts, Mr. Law calls attention to the fact that Professor Feuillerat, "than whom no man living has a more exhaustive and intimate knowledge of the Revels' Accounts in the Record Office"—an estimate with which I am in entire accord—"had previously stated that he had found Cunningham a 'most accurate' transcriber of the documents he [had] published." But this is an opinion which I cannot accept. Mr. Law himself makes mention of the fact that Cunningham omitted "two notes, one in Latin, for the auditor, stating how much had been paid on account, and how much was still due to the Master."[4] These "two notes," in reality two paragraphs, constituting more than eleven lines at the bottom of page 2 A, are at least as important as some of the trivial items about "Ivy Bayes," "nayles," "Taffutie," "Thred," "Cord," "Gravell," "Pack-

thred," "A Courten of darnex," etc. As regards punctuation, spelling, and capitalization, Cunningham was a most unreliable transcriber. Now and then he omitted words (*e.g.*, "Caled" in 3 A 15); he distorted dozens of others (*e.g.*, "lodginge" for "lodinge," "attendaunces" for "attenddendaunces," "shoes" for "thoes," and for "shows," "darnep" for "darnex," "Groieme" for "Groume," and "Wages" for "wagesses"); and he made no mention of erased lines and corrections or alterations in the originals, etc. Memoranda by the auditor—*e.g.*, that one about the names of the plays being expressed—are not only omitted, but not even mentioned in his notes. And neither Professor Feuillerat nor Mr. Law, apparently, has noticed that Cunningham omitted a long marginal note on page 7 A and—what is of even greater importance—the two signed statements, bearing the ostensible signatures of Edmund Tyllney and Thomas Flemyng, on page 9 A, as well as the date on page 1 B. These are enough, I think, to prove that Cunningham's integrity as a transcriber of official documents cannot be invoked in the defense of the impugned papers.[5]

9. One of the strongest arguments in support of the genuineness of the 1604-5 Accounts is Malone's statement in volume 2 of the 1821 *Variorum*, that "we *know* that it [*Othello*] was acted in 1604;" so far as we know, he could have based his assertion only on these Accounts, even though he has nowhere mentioned them. But the argument is by no means conclusive. Malone probably had some other source of information—nay, must have had. All the pertinent facts con-

sidered, especially Malone's failure to specify the exact date—November 1, 1604 —it seems much more likely that the forger based the *Othello* item on information he obtained from Malone. The forger thought it advisable to improve on his source. Collier, we know, was thoroughly familiar with Malone and often quoted Malone's work when defending himself against the charges of his accusers.[6]

When we recall that in 1836 Collier published a forged document which was intended to prove that *Othello* was acted before Queen Elizabeth and her Court at Harefield in 1602, we cannot but think that the item in the Accounts of 1604-5 was manufactured to corroborate in some measure Collier's earlier forgery. In fact, the frequency with which these Accounts tend to bear out a number of Collier's guesses and conjectures is one of the suspicious features about them. Thus, for example, we have here confirmation of Collier's conjecture that *Greene's Tu Quoque* originally had a different title (*cf. Extracts*, p. 226).[7]

10. That Malone had also come across the 1611-12 list has been inferred from his statement, in his privately printed *Account of the . . . Tempest* (1809), that *The Tempest* had been "performed before the middle of 1611." On what evidence he based this very circumstantial statement has not been discovered. His editor, Boswell, gives us no information on the subject and makes no reference to the existence among Malone's papers of any memoranda or transcripts which would warrant the belief that Malone had any knowledge of the 1605 or 1612 Accounts. Notwithstanding this, some scholars think that Malone's statement implies

knowledge of the data contained in the 1612 list. Malone's statement (*Variorum*, 1821, vol. 3, p. 409) that he knew of no Elizabethan Revels Accounts subsequent to those of 1588 is proof enough that when he wrote that particular chapter the Accounts of 1605 and 1612 were unknown to him. He was not the man to have left them unmentioned had he known of their existence. Knowing that George Steevens and George Chalmers were constantly on the hunt for new data concerning Shakspere, he would not have risked their discovering these Accounts and anticipating him in the publication of the date of *Measure for Measure*. (In volume 2 of his *Variorum*, 1821, p. 387, he says only that *Measure for Measure* "was written before 1607.") He would not have deferred announcing to the world a discovery which confirmed his guess (*Variorum*, 1821, vol. 2, p. 463) that *The Winter's Tale* was probably licensed in the latter part of 1610 or the beginning of 1611. That Malone was not free from the form of vanity which goes with the distinction of priority, we know from his anxiety[8] to have his essay on *The Tempest* printed almost immediately on the publication of Mr. Douce's *Illustrations of Shakespeare* (1807).

Malone's statement (in 1809!) that *The Tempest* was "performed *before the middle* of 1611" (whereas the Revels Accounts only mention a performance at Court on November 1, 1611) seems fairly conclusive evidence, even without the previous considerations, that his assertion was not based on the 1611-12 pamphlet,[9] if we may call it that. Of course he might have said more than was warranted by the evidence in his possession; it was, however, not like Malone to do that. Fortunately, it is now possible to offer an explanation for this apparently insoluble problem: Malone discovered all or parts of a Revels Book for 1611-12 after he had published his essay on *The Tempest*. (See p. 21.)

11. Returning to the suspected play-lists, we note that the 1604-5 Book has the surname of Heywood ("Hewood") once (as the author of a lost play, *How to Larne of a woman to wooe*—if there ever was such a play [10]), Chapman once (as the author of *All Foulles*, a play in which Collier seems to have been unduly interested [11]), and "Shaxberd" four times, though there are eight entries of plays by Shakspere. Ben Jonson's name is not given at all, though two of his plays are included in the list. The omission of Jonson's name and the mention of Shakspere's name only four times was, it seems to me, contrived by the forger for a definite purpose, viz., to cover up the fact that he could not give the name of the author of the unknown and non-extant play, *The Spanish Maze*.

12. This item—*A Tragid[ye]e of the Spainsh[e] Maz*—is of very great interest: not only does it present us with a tell-tale ghostly *ye* at the end of the word "Tragide" (*cf.* p. 39) and a pale and unobliterated *e* in "Spainshe" [*sic*], but it shows that the forger had originally written a name in the column reserved for the names of "The poets" and had subsequently erased this both by rubbing and chemically. (For an explanation of these phenomena, see later.) Mr. Law's

facsimile (*q.v.*) shows this erasure clearly, and a photograph by transmitted light shows the paper at this spot to be almost as translucent as tissue paper, as a result of the severe rubbing. [12] (See facsimile 13 *b*.)

Such a thorough erasure, so evidently calculated to obliterate all traces of the matter written, in a document in which it would have been sufficient to cross out the objectionable name, especially as the names of the dramatists were of no consequence, is almost *per se* conclusive evidence of forgery.

13. Another extremely suspicious feature in the external appearance of these papers is the evidence furnished by pages 3 A and 4 A that the scrivener was trying to follow, line for line, a copy or model lying before him. The page had clearly been ruled off before he began to make his entries. Our penman evidently wrote a slightly larger hand than could be accommodated in the space at his disposal. And so we find him huddling together, almost inextricably, the letters of the last word in a number of lines (viz., 3A10, 3A11, 3A14, 4A1, 4A19), though he had space enough at his disposal for additional lines. Such an absurd procedure, I need hardly say, is practically inconceivable in a genuine document.

14. Perhaps the strongest argument in support of the genuineness of the Cunningham papers is that which was recently urged by that fine Irish scholar, Mr. William J. Lawrence. [13] He points out (*op. cit.*, p. 31) that in the 1612 play-list "a playe called Himens Holiday" ("A Play Called Himens Ho[a]lliday") is said to have been acted by the Duke of York's Players, and that in 1842 no

one living could have assigned the non-extant *Hymen's Holiday* to that troupe, inasmuch as it was only in 1849 that the Rev. Frederick Gard Fleay "proved" that this play had been written by William Rowley, one of the original patentees of the Duke's Players in 1610. But, as a matter of fact, Fleay had *not* proved that William Rowley was the author of this play. Fleay's argument[14] is only that if *Hymen's Holiday* was played by the Duke of York's Company at Court in 1612 (of which company William Rowley was a member), then the Rowley who wrote the play was, in all probability, William. But since there is not a particle of unquestioned evidence extant to connect the play with the Duke of York's Players, and since, on the contrary, we have reason to believe that this company did not play "before the Kings Matie,"[15] Mr. Fleay can really not be said to have demonstrated the true authorship of *Hymen's Holiday*.

All that can logically be said is that it is curious, if nothing else, that the forger should have associated a play by a Rowley with the Duke of York's Players at a time (1842) when it seems not to have been known that either Samuel or William Rowley belonged to that organization. The forger may have made a lucky guess, or he may have known of the existence of the patent of March 30, 1610, which was first printed in extenso by Mr. T. E. Tomlins in the *Shakespeare Society Papers*, 1849, vol. 4, pp. 47-49. That Collier may have known more about this company than he printed is rendered probable by the fact, apparently unknown even to modern delvers into the history of

Elizabethan theatrical companies, that a "license" to the Duke of York's servants, issued "in the ninth [*sic*] year of James I," was published by "A. J. K." in *The Gentleman's Magazine* in March, 1840[16] (vol. 13, n. s., p. 268). Just when Mr. Tomlins rediscovered this document, which he erroneously designated as a "privy seal," is unknown. Cunningham is said by Mr. Wood—erroneously, I think—to have "discovered his documents in 1834," though he did not publish them till 1842. Or—an alternative theory—the forger may have decided to bring the Duke of York's Company into his papers because of the then recently announced discovery concerning that organization. If a 1611-12 book or fragment, discovered by Malone after 1809 and by Cunningham sometime before 1842, contained a list of plays, there is no reason why *Hymen's Holiday* may not have been included in that list.

15. If it be true, as Mrs. Stopes contends,—and it certainly seems to be so—that on January 12, 1612, the Prince was *in London* and attended a performance by the Duke of York's Players there that night, then the entry in these Accounts which says that the Queen's Players and the King's Players played *The Silver Age* before the Queen and the Prince *at Greenwich* on January 12 must be a fabrication.[17]

16. In the essay previously referred to, Mr. Lawrence advances an argument in the defense of Cunningham which I do not quite understand. He shows that the suspected forger's knowledge was not only not ahead of his times but not even abreast with them. In the *Extracts*

from the Accounts (1842, p. xl), Cunningham identifies *the prowde Mayde* (played before the King on Tuesday, February 25, 1612), a Lady Elizabeth's Men's play, with Beaumont and Fletcher's *The Maid's Tragedy*, "though he [Cunningham] should have known [says Mr. Lawrence] that the latter ... belonged to the King's Men." Mr. Lawrence seemingly wishes us to infer that a forger would have been careful not to make the mistake of saying anything contrary to ascertained knowledge; and that since Cunningham did make a mistake, he could not have been a forger. This is very much like Mr. Lawrence's assertion that it is the "much blazoned discrepancy between the Revels Accounts of 1604-5 and 1611-12 and the correlative warrants issued by the Treasurer of the Chamber" which largely assures him that "the alleged Cunningham forgeries are wholly genuine." But this proposition seems to me no less untenable than it would be to maintain that a document is a forgery because it is free from errors. To explain the mistake of identifying *the prowde Mayde*, as the name is given in the Treasurer's warrant, with *the proud Mayds Tragedie*, as it is designated in 3B19, we need only remember that forgers sometimes fall into their own traps. The addition of the word "Tragedie" to the title found in the warrant was undoubtedly due to the forger's desire—for reasons of his own—to make the identification with Beaumont and Fletcher's exquisite masterpiece more certain. To me, "proud" is the most unfitting adjective that could have been applied to the alternately chastened and brazen Evadne.

But Mr. Lawrence's argument is open to a far more fatal objection: He assumes, on Cunningham's authority, that *the proud Mayds Tragedie* was verily Beaumont and Fletcher's great drama; Mr. Fleay and Sir Edmund Chambers, on the contrary, are inclined to believe—on very insufficient grounds, I think—that it was Middleton's *A Chaste Maid in Cheapside*, which was a Lady Elizabeth's Men's play. Mr. Chambers[18] makes no mention of Cunningham's wild guess.[19]

17. A most plausible argument in favor of the genuineness of the indicted play-lists is embodied in the following quotation from Mr. Lawrence's defense of Cunningham: "The question has to be asked, Why did Cunningham write *The Moor of Venis*[20] instead of *Othello?* How many Shakespearean scholars today are aware that, the titling of Q1 and of the Folio play nothwithstanding, the tragedy was commonly known[21] and regularly acted throughout the first half of the seventeenth century as *The Moor of Venice?*"

The only objection to this argument is that it is questionable whether, on the basis of extant evidence—a memorandum by the Prince of Wirtemberg's secretary and another one by Mr. Mildmay—it is permissible to say that this play was "commonly known and regularly acted" as *The Moor of Venice*.[22] In all other references but one (to be discussed below), official as well as printed, the play is called *Othello* or *Orthello*. Pepys, we may recall, records having read *Othello, Moor of Venice*, on August 20, 1666; and there is absolutely no reason why the acting-name of the play should have been changed after the middle of the seventeenth century. A play with a double name might very well be spoken of by either one of its titles. Thus, for example, in the Rawlinson (or Vertue) Manuscript (*MS. Rawl. A. 239/47*) a play called *S* *John ffalstafe* is said to have been performed before "the Princes Highnes" in 1613, and there is no way of knowing whether this meant *II Henry IV* or *The Merry Wives of Windsor*. In the same manuscript John Heminges is paid for the performance of a play called *The Hotspur* (presumably *I Henry IV*), another called *Caesars Tragedye* (presumably *Julius Caesar*), "And one other called *Benedicte and Betteris*" (presumably *Much Ado about Nothing*). No one, I think, would say that this warrants the opinion that these plays were "commonly known and regularly acted" by these names.

Any significance which the Mildmay entry and the Wirtemberg entry might otherwise have is completely offset, in my opinion, by the fact that in the precious Rawlinson Manuscript, with which the forger surely was acquainted (it is referred to by Malone), and which could have furnished him with the names of many of the plays he included in the impugned Accounts, Shakspere's great play is called *The Moore of Venice*. The forger therefore had at least one known precedent.[23]

That Collier was acquainted with and interested in the alternative title of Shakspere's tragedy is established beyond a doubt by the fact that in 1841 —the date should be noted—he published, in his *Memoirs of Edward Alleyn*, a fraudulent version of an entry in the Dulwich College Manuscripts, which now reads, according to Sir George F. Warner : "5. i blew damask cote the More in Venus." The manuscript, before Collier tampered with it, read only "5. i blew damask cote the moro." (*Cf.* Sir George's *Catalogue of the Manuscripts and Muniments of Alleyn's College*, 1881, p. 21.) That Collier had *Othello* in mind we know from his statement (*Memoirs*, p. 18) that "the Moore in Venis [as he there prints the words, *op. cit.*, p. 20] may have been another version of *Othello*."

18. The 1612 play-list records a performance "By the Queens players and the Kings men" of Heywood's *The Siluer Aiedg* on January 12 "at Grinwidge." Mr. Lawrence finds significance in the fact that Cunningham, the suspected forger, "when writing his notes in his book, *Extracts* (etc.), made no attempt to elucidate so uncommon and puzzling an entry." From the address to the reader in the 1632 Quarto of *The Iron Age* we know—but Cunningham, says Mr. Lawrence, evidently did not—that "These *Ages* . . . were . . . often . . . Acted by two Companies vppon one Stage at once." Notwithstanding his ignorance of this, Cunningham is supposed to have forged an item in which it is alleged that two companies played *The Silver Age* at Greenwich! Two considerations, however, serve to dispose of this argument: (1) Cunningham's silence does not prove "that the item had baffled him." He, or his principal, may have decided to say nothing about the address prefixed to *The Iron Age*, so as not to betray the source of his information. (2) Collier, we may be sure, was thoroughly familiar with the Epistles in *The Iron Age* (1632).

19. A much more important argument is embodied in a footnote on pp. 30-31 of Mr. Lawrence's essay, in which it is pointed out that on the flyleaf of Malone's copy of *The Silver Age* (Q. 1613), now preserved in the Bodleian, occurs the following memorandum in Malone's hand: "This play was performed at Greenwich before the King and Queen 'by the Queen's Players and the King's Men' in Jany 1611-12 *as appears from the Accounts of Sir George Buc*, Master of the Revels." Malone must, therefore, Mr. Lawrence concludes, have seen this Revels Book. But the reader must note that Malone's memorandum does not assign an *exact date* to the performance, and that, while he asserts that the performance was given *before the King and Queen*, the forger says "before the Queen and the Prince."

In view of the fact that Malone gives George Buc's accounts as the source for his knowledge that *The Silver Age* was played in January, 1612, and in view of the further fact that we now have reason for considering certain parts of the impugned books to be genuine, we must conclude—as was pointed out in my discussion of *The Tempest*—that sometime after 1809 Malone discovered part or all of a genuine Book of Accounts for 1611-12. That his editor, Boswell, said nothing about this Revels Book may have been due to the fact that Malone either had not made a transcript of it or had lost or mislaid his transcript. Malone's error—if error it be—about the King's absence from the performance, and the Prince's presence there, may therefore be easily explained on the theory that for these details Malone was relying on his memory. It will be noted, by the way, that he has quotation marks only before and after the words "by the Queen's Players and the King's Men."[24] The exact date—the Sunday following Twelfth Night—found in the questioned play-list most likely emanated from the forger's desire to be more specific than his original—perhaps to give it greater verisimilitude. That in doing this he blundered is clearly established by two facts: (1) In the Declared Accounts of the Treasurer of the Chamber there is no record of a payment to either the Queen's Men or the King's Men for a performance on January 12, 1612. (2) On the day mentioned in the play-list the Prince was witnessing a performance in London, not at Greenwich.

20. Having hitherto limited myself to a consideration and refutation of the arguments brought forward in favor of the genuineness of the questioned documents, I shall now propose some positive arguments against the genuineness of the Cunningham papers. In the 1611-12 list we are told that on November 5, 1611, the King's Players enacted a play called "ye Winters nights Tayle," presumably Shakspere's[25] *The Winter's Tale.* Mr. Law, noticing the departure of the list from other notices of Shakspere's play, says (SSF, pp. 78-79) that we have here "a version of its title [which was] presumably furnished to the Master by Shakespeare's Company, if not by [the poet] himself. Though formed," he continues, "apparently as a sort of balance or contrast to *A Midsummer Night's Dream*—just as Shakespeare's original title for *Othello* was [?] *The Moor of Venice*, in contrast to *The Merchant*

of *Venice*—it has a significance of some import. For it helps to confute the contentions of some critics that the play received its name because of its plot being a 'wintry one'; or because of its having been produced in the winter season—an idea of Halliwell-Phillips's [*sic*]. It has, on the contrary," he goes on to say, "lately been made pretty clear that it was called *The Winter's Tale* for the reason, emphasized by Shakespeare himself three or four times in the course of the dialogue—as has been pointed out by M. Jusserand in his admirable essay on the play . . .— because it was just such a fanciful romantic piece, full of strange happenings and wonders and improbabilities, as was then known as *A Winter's Tale*, or an *Old Wives' Tale*, told round the fire on a winter's night. Hence the significance of the word *night* in its title as given in Buc's Revels Book —a unique variation which reinforces M. Jesserand's [*sic*] argument."

Notwithstanding Mr. Law's exposition, I am quite sure that Shakspere's play was never, except in these forged documents, known by the uneuphonious name, *The Winter's Night's Tale* (Mr. Law's version).

That Shakspere's play was from the very first known as *The Winter's Tale*, and not as *The Winter's Night's Tale*, is inferable from the following evidence: (1) In a manuscript entry in Dr. Simon Forman's famous and invaluable *Booke of Plaies* (first published in 1836) we are told that on the 15th of May, 1611, he witnessed a performance of "the Winters Talle at the glob." (2) An entry, dated August 19, 1623, in the Office-Book of Sir Henry Herbert, Master of the Revels

to James the First, reads: "For the Kings players. An olde playe called Winters Tale, formerly allowed of by Sir George Bucke." (3) An entry in *MS. Rawlinson A. 239* informs us that "The Winters Tale" was acted at Court in 1613. (For a transcript of this very important document, see Appendix B.)

21. Having nothing new to contribute to the much discussed, indefinite, and anomalous entry of a performance of "A play of Loues Labours Lost" "Betwin Newers Day And Twelfe day" (recorded on 3 A), I shall merely refer the reader to the writings of Mr. Law, Mrs. Stopes, and Sir Edmund Chambers. In a letter to me Mr. Lawrence concedes that the entry is perplexing and thus far inexplicable, whether we regard it as genuine or as a forgery.[26]

22. Mrs. Stopes has made it quite clear,[27] from a careful comparison of these play-lists with the official Accounts of the Treasurer of the Chamber, that these play-lists are defective, suspiciously defective, in many respects, and anomalous in others. She has also shown that Cunningham's play-lists do not distinguish between day and night performances, although the Declared Accounts (which, presumably, were based on these) do; that the locale of the performances is incorrectly given in the play-lists (*e.g.*, these say that *The Moor of Veins* was played in "the Banketinge house," whereas the Lord Chamberlain's Accounts designate "the Greate Chamber" as the place of performance); that the play-lists omit performances recorded elsewhere; that they err in the correct designation of the Choristers of the Chapel (who performed on January 3,

1604-5); and that they record a performance on a day when none was
given. These objections have never been
met successfully.

Mr. Lawrence, it is true, has argued,
very shrewdly, that the errors and inconsistencies which Mrs. Stopes has pointed
out prove the documents genuine; he
thinks it unlikely that Cunningham, if
he were the forger, would have failed
to check up his fabrication with all the
data at his disposal, notably the Declared
Accounts which he published (with the
Revels Accounts) in 1842. He says: "A
forger would surely have taken care
that all the dates were in harmony,
that there should be sound equivalence."

It must be granted that a forger
would be expected to do his work carefully and with the application of common
sense, if common sense would permit
one to perpetrate a forgery. But we all
know that forgers, like other criminals,
almost never succeed in eliminating all
clues. That even so shrewd and accom-
plished a forger as John Payne Collier
was guilty of the most absurdly stupid
blunders will be apparent when it is re-
called that in the "Perkins Folio" he left
penciled letters and words in his own
handwriting underneath his inked imitation of Old English writing; that he
prepared a forged document on paper
of a date later than the time to which
the document professed to belong;[28] and
that he fabricated legal and official documents in the same hand in which the
notes in the "Perkins Folio" were written.
He also attempted to utter as a genuine
old document a fabrication "written on
paper with a gilt edge, apparently a leaf
cut from a book" (Wheatley, p. 57); and

in one instance even had the effrontery
to read words into a genuine document,
convinced apparently that no one would
ever take the trouble to read the original.

That we may hear no more of the
argument that inconsistencies, errors,
and contradictions may be proofs of
genuineness—and to give a striking illus-
tration of how absurdly a forger may
operate—I shall recapitulate here, briefly,
Mr. Thomas J. Wise's account of a printed
forgery by Collier in a copy of Chapman's play, *All Fools*. (See my comments
on *All Foulles*, pp. 28, 75.) In the 1825
edition of Dodsley's *Select Collection of
Old Plays*, Collier, one of the editors,
printed a dedicatory sonnet to Sir Thomas
Walsingham in the reprint of the 1605
Quarto of *All Fools*. This sonnet is to
be found only in a single copy of the
Quarto.[29] Fortunately Mr. Wise located
this very copy and was able to prove,[30]
without any difficulty, that the poem
is "a palpable forgery" and was printed
on an inserted [!] leaf. The paper is of
the period. The extraordinary feature
of this forgery is that a man so gifted
and brilliant as Collier undoubtedly was,
should have been so stupid as to have
printed a forged poem on a leaf of paper
which was small, damaged, and soiled,
and to have inserted it between two
leaves which were larger, clean, and
fresh. And—even more astounding—
he took the trouble to "extend" the
margins of the inserted leaf to the size
of its neighbors. A man who had the
skill and the patience and the monomania to plan and execute such forgeries,
and yet was stupid enough to be guilty
of such blunders, could indeed have
concocted and fabricated the many-

errored Revels Accounts. That it *was* he I shall show in a subsequent chapter.

23. It has not heretofore been noted that one of the two paragraphs which Cunningham omitted in his transcript seemingly contradicts a statement in another part of the Book. At the bottom of page 2 A (*cf.* facsimile 2) we are told that the "Surplusage" (= balance) of the Master's "Accompt for the year ended the last of October: 1604:" amounted to "Threscore six poundes nyne shillinges ten pence," but at the top of page 9 A the balance due to the Master is "Threscore ffifti[e]ne poundes ffive Shillinges tow pence." This discrepancy is the more remarkable because the amount mentioned on page 2 A tallies with the privy seal at the Public Record Office (*E* 403/2561, *fo.63*). That there is something queer about these omitted paragraphs is evident from the fact that the second one begins with the word "But," as if there were some opposition between it and the contents of the (Latin) paragraph preceding it.[31]

24. In Book B, page 7, the Master of the Revels presents a bill for £280, 7s. 0d., whereas the privy seal (*P. R.*, *Exchequer* 403/2701), dated December 30, 1612, authorizes the Treasurer and Chamberlain to pay £220, 7s. 0d.—a difference of £60. This discrepancy is explainable only on the theory that the forger had no knowledge of this privy seal's existence. Part of the book of privy seals for 1612, I am reliably informed (by Miss Phina Schrader, of London), is missing.

25. At the foot of 2 A the accountant says that the "M[aste]r of the Revelles [Edmund Tyllney] ... *was payed* ... the S[u]rplusage of his Accompt for the year

ended the last of October: 1604," but at the top of the ninth page of the same Book, and as an after-addition, "the said M[aste]r of the Revell[es] *demandeth Allowaunce* for the S[u]rplusage of his last Accompte." This may be the reason why Cunningham omitted to print the perplexing paragraphs at the bottom of page 2 A and at the top of 9 A.

The facts we have been considering, including the many errors and omissions, the inconsistencies between these papers and other sources of information, the contradictions in the papers themselves, the uncertainties about the spelling of even quite simple words (*e.g.*, "double," "prize," "like," "four," "were," "called"), and so forth, amply warrant us in concluding that the Books of Accounts, as we now have them, are not exact copies of genuine originals for the years in question (1604-5 and 1611-12).

In what has preceded I have given reasons for thinking that some sort of Revels Accounts for the years 1604-5 and 1611-12 had been discovered a year or two before Malone's death and rediscovered shortly before 1842. But it is not impossible that they had not been rediscovered at all: Collier or Cunningham or both might simply have noticed that these books of Jacobean Revels had not attracted any attention from students of theatrical history. The older of the two men, already experienced in the art of literary forgery, saw here an opportunity to bolster up some of his theories, fortify some of his guesses, disprove some of the conjectures of his predecessors, and show to the world how popular Shakspere had been at the Court of King James. For reasons which we cannot even pretend to guess, the younger man—a clever and probably very vain youngster, barely out of his teens—assented to participate in what he may have regarded as a clever hoax and to play the rôle of discoverer. The details having been arranged, they set to work. When it was possible to do so, they used the leaves or sheets of the genuine books; what they lacked, they made up from older bundles. So much of the original paper as did not serve their purpose, they destroyed. And this was Cunningham's "little Guanahana."

CHAPTER FIVE

THE WRITING

WHERE, as in the present instance, a document as a whole is under suspicion of being a forgery and the question is not whether the forgery was perpetrated by a certain person whose genuine and ordinary handwriting is available for comparison, the investigator's task is more than ordinarily difficult. In such cases the examiner subjects to the most searching scrutiny the paper, watermarks, ink, wording, folding, style or system of writing, etc. In the case of the suspected Revels Accounts the paper and the watermarks are not elements in the investigation, since genuine paper of the period was easily accessible to the forger. The ink has already been discussed. Notwithstanding many obvious difficulties, the forged character of the Cunningham documents can fortunately be established by the writing itself.

In January, 1869, a writer in *The British Quarterly Review* asserted that "it only required *a glance* of the experts to discover that the list of Shakespeare's plays ... had been appended to the old documents by a modern hand." From this it might be inferred that the differences in the writing between the two lists and the rest of the documents were so glaring that the experts of that day should have rejected the documents as

not being the genuine product of a Revels clerk of the Jacobean era. Mr. Bond, Assistant Keeper of Manuscripts at the British Museum, is on record as having said that he saw "reasons for doubting the genuineness of one, at least, of these papers, from the peculiar character of the writing and the spelling." Sir Frederic Madden pronounced the play-list of 1604-5 a "forgery, a gross forgery, from beginning to end." So far as we can tell now, everyone who examined—*i.e.*, looked at or scrutinized—the documents "at once" declared the earlier play-list "a palpable forgery," whereas concerning the later play-list (that of 1611-12) condemnation was not so general.

Having subjected the impugned pages to a close scrutiny, Mr. Law thought he found, to his great surprise, that they had not been fairly dealt with by the early experts and scholars, that there seemed to be "but little wrong with the form and shape of the letters," that to the ordinary eye the ink in the play-lists and in the rest of the documents seemed to be identical, and that there was nowhere "any indication of preparatory pencillings, *nor any sign of any sort of tampering*."[1]

Thereupon Mr. Law decided to get the opinions of modern experts. Doctor

C. W. Wallace, "Associate Professor of English Language and Literature in the University of Nebraska, the well-known scholar," accordingly examined *the play-lists* "with great care" (but presumably without a microscope, without the aid of photographic enlargements, and without making chemical tests) and "unhesitatingly confirmed the writer's [Mr. Law's] view that each is exactly what it purports to be, that they are both absolutely genuine, and that there is not a scrap of anything modern or forged about either of them." It is greatly to be regretted that Mr. Law did not elicit from Professor Wallace a statement of the specific characteristics of forgery and modernity which he looked for but did not discover. Without such a statement his opinion is worth as much, or as little, as that of the early experts whom Mr. Law denounces so vigorously and justly.[2]

Because of the obvious and astounding differences of opinion between the experts of the nineteenth century and those consulted by Mr. Law, it may at this point be as well, perhaps, to ask the reader to examine the facsimile of page 3 of the Revels Accounts for 1604-5 (*i. e.*, 3A) and to note its obviously "fishy" appearance. Mr. Wood, we may recall, speaks of the "woolly" appearance of the writing. By "woolly" he means nothing more nor less than that the writing does not seem to be sharply defined: the edges of the pen strokes are hazy, blurry, as if the flow of ink had extended slightly beyond the grooves made by the nibs of the pen, or the writing had been "blotted" by an absorbent of poor quality which did

not take the ink quickly enough and therefore caused it to spread. (See facsimile 3.)

Another conspicuous feature in the suspected pages is a certain unnatural appearance about the writing as a whole —an appearance which suggests, to one experienced in studying documents, that the writing was done slowly, laboriously, hesitatingly, as if the penman had been copying from a model, making mistakes (omitting letters) and attempting to correct them. This *test of general appearance* or pictorial effect is perfectly legitimate if one is acquainted with the style of writing involved and with other documents of the same kind and of the same, or approximately the same, period. That the reader may judge for himself as to this, let him compare facsimile 3 with facsimile 9—the latter a facsimile of a page of the Revels Accounts for 1587-88. That the questioned play-list was written much more slowly and deliberately than the unquestioned writing is evident. In a routine official document of no consequence, as this one was, such slow, labored, hesitant, and studied writing may safely be set down as a forgery or as an imitation. Other evidences of forgery will be specified later. Professor Wallace's opinion is, therefore, not borne out by an examination of the writing.

But Mr. Law did not rest his case on the opinion of Professor Wallace alone. He consulted Sir George Warner, Keeper of Manuscripts at the British Museum, who examined the writing "closely" (again without the aforementioned aids: a microscope, photographic enlargements, etc.). After a "prolonged and

(33)

searching scrutiny" Sir George pointed out "many little features which told strongly in favor" of the papers, though he admitted that on a first glance the two 1604-5 play-lists had "a somewhat suspicious air about them." "Finally he declared that he could detect no sign of any modern fabrication at all, nor even any tampering with the manuscripts; and that he saw no reason whatever for supposing that the lists were not, in every regard, absolute [*sic*] genuine writings of the early seventeenth century."

In view of their suspicious appearance and the general condemnation passed upon the documents by the early investigators, how is it possible, the reader is sure to ask, for a paleographer of Sir George's eminence to have committed himself so unequivocally to their authenticity without specifying the marks of genuineness upon which he relied for his verdict? The answer to this question is twofold:

1. Sir George is, notwithstanding his eminence as a paleographer, not a bibliotist (an expert in the art of detecting forgery and of identifying penmen from their calligraphic peculiarities). To be able to decipher and read ancient documents and to assign them to their period is very different from determining the genuineness or spuriousness of a questioned document and identifying the individual who wrote it. A paleographer may know nothing of bibliotics, and a bibliotist may know nothing of paleography.

2. Sir George's eyesight may not have been equal to the task. In response to an inquiry concerning this matter, a few years ago, Sir George kindly informed me that he was then, in 1924, an old man (*aet.* eighty years), that his eyesight had become so poor that he could not re-examine the documents. It seems to me eminently reasonable to infer from this that when he examined the documents for Mr. Law his eyesight may not have been of the best. How else can we account for the fact that he not only did not see the evidences of forgery which I have already pointed out and others which are to follow, but that he also overlooked some of the forgeries in Henslowe's *Diary*?[3]

Not wholly undaunted by the array of learned men—all experts and all unbiased—whom Mr. Law summoned in corroboration of his opinion on the Cunningham papers, Mrs. Stopes ("Audi Alteram Partem," *pseud.*) attacked the verdict and the papers in several letters to *The Athenæum* in 1911 (vol. 1, p. 638; vol. 2, pp. 101, 131, 421) and 1912 (vol. 1, pp. 469, 654; vol. 2, p. 412). Mr. Law thereupon replied to his opponent's criticism of the experts and of the papers in a series of letters (in the same periodical[4]) and in a second book, *More about Shakespeare Forgeries* (London, 1913), in which he seemingly completely demolished her case on the historical side. As regards Mrs. Stopes's strictures on the ink and the penmanship, he contented himself—as was to be expected—with appealing to "the reasoned opinions of such well-known paleographers as Sir George Warner, Sir Henry Maxwell-Lyte," etc.

But Mrs. Stopes was right. She charged —correctly—that the writer of the play-lists was nothing but a poor "copyist," one "whose eye knew the forms of the letters of the times, but [whose hand muscles] had not been trained to obey the dictates of his eye," whose "tremulous pen occasionally slips" and who, "to hide this, trims his letters at abnormal points"; who "did not know how to... hold his hand for that style of writing" and "had often to stop and paint his letters," etc. In the remaining pages of this chapter I shall apply myself to proving the correctness of Mrs. Stopes's allegations and charges.

If there is any one argument that Mr. Law invokes and relies on more insistently than that based on the Dobbie report, it is this: that *the suspected play-lists, even those of 1604-5, show not the slightest evidence of tampering*. The experts he consulted evidently all agreed with him as to this; not one of them said a word that might be construed as anything but agreement with his opinion. And yet they are all—Dr. Wallace, Sir George, Sir Henry, Mr. Law, etc.—greatly in error. So conspicuous and so gross are the evidences of tampering —even in the supposedly genuine play-list of 1611-12—that one wonders whether the investigators ever really looked at these papers, or, if they did so, how they escaped the instant and final conviction that the papers are such clumsy forgeries as to make it incomprehensible that an intelligent person had ever attempted to palm them off as genuine.

In the play-list of 1611-12 (*cf.* fac-simile 6) we have the following perfectly obvious evidences of tampering:

In the word "Called," in the fifth line, the second *l* was evidently inserted after the word "Caled" had been written by the scribe. This *l* was made with a different pen and with different (paler) ink. Surely, such a correction of the spelling of so simple a word in a document of no consequence, written in an era when penmen had the utmost latitude regarding orthography, even with proper names, is an instance of gross tampering. In the very next line we have an identical intrusion of a second *l* in the same word. Also in the seventh line. Also in the eighth line. And in the ninth line (in "called"). In the tenth line it is the first *l* in "Called" that was added as a correction; also in the twelfth line. In the sixteenth, seventeenth, eighteenth, and nineteenth lines the correction is the second *l*.

What makes this tampering with the word "Called" even more remarkable is the fact that in the 1604-5 play-list the same scribe had written indifferently "Called," "Caled," and "Cauled." Just what object the forger could have had in doubling the *l*'s in the later play-list is subject only to conjecture. From the fact that in Book A he had written "the play *of* Henry the fift," "A Tragide *of* the Spainshe Maz," "A play *of* the Marthant of Veins [*sic*]," "A play *of* the Merry Wiues of Winsor," "The Plaie *of*: Errors," and "A play *of* Loues Labours Lost," whereas in Book B he had always (five times) written "A play *called*" so-and-so, I think it reasonable to guess that he wished to imply that the scribe had become more modern in the intervening years. This sort of supersubtlety the madness of forgery often hits on.

Another noteworthy fact regarding this scribe's (according to Mr. Law an "illiterate scribe's") punctiliousness in the spelling of the word "Called" is his writing "Duck" for *Duke*, "Grinwidg" for *Greenwich*, "Aiedg" for *Age*, "woere" for *were*, etc. Incidentally it may be remarked that some of these spellings, and others which I shall point out, are very suggestive of the mock antique of a forger. And it may safely be set down as a rule that a document in which simple words, *e. g.*, *like*, *called*, *played*, and *double*, are spelled differently almost every time they occur, is a forgery. The more nearly illiterate an Elizabethan was, the more unlikely he was to vary his spelling.

The intruded *l*'s are not the only evidence of tampering to be found in the 1612 play-list. Above the word "Called" in lines 5, 7, 8, 9, 10, 12, and 18, the reader will notice a semilunar or semicircular curve (resembling a sickle without a handle) which surely was made after the completion of the document and with the same writing materials[5] with which the fraudulent and unnecessary *l*'s were made. Considering that these interpolated *l*'s were probably not made by the penman who wrote the bulk of the documents—as may be inferred from the fact that not only these *l*'s but other interpolated letters differ from the other writing in pen pressure, shading, line quality, and slant—it seems to me impossible to account for these curves on any other hypothesis than that two persons were engaged in the forgery and that one of them, dissatisfied with the work of his associate, went over the completed work, making certain corrections and indicating other points which would have to be altered in a later, revised and corrected, copy.

Not impossibly someone may bring forward the hypothesis that the interpolated *l*'s and curves may be the work of some person who handled the documents after they left Cunningham's hands.[6] Fortunately, there is abundant evidence to disprove such an assumption. The presence of other interpolations, which Cunningham incorporated in his transcript of these play-lists[7] and which were written in the same ink and with the same pen and by the same hand that wrote the *l*'s (Cunningham spells "Called" with double *l*), proves that the tampering was done before Cunningham's book was published. The previous paragraph has prepared us for an examination of other interpolations and tamperings on this page. At the end of line 13 may be seen a few letters (written with a decidedly grayish "ink")[8] which Cunningham transcribed as "High-" and which are generally rendered as "Highness," though they look much more like "Hid." What we are now concerned with is not that the scribe failed to complete the word "Highness"— though he had space enough at his disposal—but that he stopped after the word "his" (the line reads: "𝕿𝖜𝖊𝖑𝖋𝖊, Night The Princes Mask performed by Gentelmen of his") and that his associate added, with another pen and in the ink of the telltale *l*'s, the letters *H-i-d*, or whatever they may be. Note also that the peculiar attention-calling semilunar curve is to be seen also above the added "Hid." This *H*, by the way, differs from the *H*'s in the words "Himens Holiday" in line 18 as to slant, design, thickness of line, etc. And yet these things had not previously been noticed!

Other additions and corrections by another hand than the original scribe's and in the ink with which the unnecessary *l*'s, etc., were made are the second *A* in line 7 ("A play called A King & no king"), the *z* in the word "prize" (in the left margin, opposite line 14), the mark over the word "Twiñes" (for *Twins*, in line 10), and the mark over the word "run" (in the left margin, above the word "prize").

The remarkable reduplication of the abbreviating flourish above the word "Ruing" (in line 7) is another indication of tampering.

The spelling of his words caused the penman of this sheet much more concern than would have been the case with a Jacobean clerk employed by Sir George Buc. In line 18 he could not make up his mind whether he should write "Holiday" or "Haliday"; in the left margin he told us that "the King & prince, wth diuer [*sic*] of his Nobilmen did rūn at ye Ring for a price," and then he or his coadjutor changed "price" to "prize"; he changed "Nobelman" to "Nobilmen" (though in line 17 he had written "Noblman"); and "whitfriers" he altered to "whitfriars" (opposite line 11).

Another suspicious feature in this document is the occasional presence, at the end of a word, of the upper (terminal) half of what the forger seems originally to have intended for an Old English final *e*. This is strikingly shown in the words "presented" (line 3) and "Called" (line 6). It occurs frequently in the other pages of Book B—in words ending with the letter *d*: "Presented," "afforsayd," and "Allowed" on page 2; in the word "Assidew" near the bottom of

4B; in the word "land" on 5B (line 14), etc. That the final *e* troubled the scribe is manifested on almost every page. Thus, for example, on the front cover of Book B a thin, unshaded final *e* appears after the heavily shaded word "Ending" in such a manner as to leave no doubt that its survival was accidental; this is also shown in the word "belonging" in 2 B 11, and elsewhere.

The peculiarly indented *l*'s—*e.g.*, in the words "ffollowethe" and "Allso" (3 B 2)—demand our attention. It will be noticed that only the first of the two *l*'s is indented, making it appear as if this *l* stood on a stilt. Jacobean penmen made this stilt by giving the downstroke of the Old English *l*—*i.e.*, its main stem— a slight bend to the right, moving the pen down and then turning sharply up and to the right. But our forger, not having been expert at doing this, sometimes added the stilt after the letter was finished—a thing which a Jacobean penman would not have taken the trouble to do. This artificial stilt is strikingly shown in the *l* of "Tilt" in the last line of 3 B and may be seen in many places in these documents.

That the matter on this page (3 B) was originally written out in faint lines and was subsequently painted or written over with a darker fluid is shown by the occasional remnants of the original outlines. Note the double outline of the base of the *T* in "Tilt" (3 B 22), of the top of the *T* in "Tempest" (3 B 5), of the *T* in "Twiñes" (3 B 10), of the *T* in "Tu" (3 B 16), of the *l* in "Nobelmen" (left margin of 3 B), and of innumerable letters on the other pages—*e.g.*, the *R* in "Reg" (2 B 3).

In a number of instances the scribe betrays the fact that he was not familiar with the script he was overwriting. In line 20 (3 B) he put a *t* and the head of a *y* instead of *th* above the numeral ("24"). On page 4 B (line 14) he wrote "Johnd" instead of "Johns," because he mistook the faint outline of an Old English *s* for a final *d*. A little lower down on the page he began to write "soune" instead of "doune." Occasionally (*e.g.*, on page 7 A) he dropped into writing "wᵗʰ" where the text requires "wᶜʰ," or *vice versa*, and then tried to cover up his error.

That evidences of tampering occur on pages other than 3 B goes almost without saying. Thus, for example, on 5 B the word "kandelsticks" (in Old English script) is doctored—for the sake of variety, probably—into "Candelsticks" and "doble" (line 4) is changed into the more archaic "dobell." The word "double" troubled this scribe elsewhere too: on page 4 B he could not decide either for "dobel" or "dobble," and so he gave us a combination of all three. It may perhaps be mentioned here as a curious "coincidence" that Collier's manuscript book of *Emendations* to Elizabethan plays presents the same bungling uncertainty about the spelling of the word "double."

And, furthermore, there is hardly a line or a word in which there are not evidences of tremor, hesitation, patching, and mending—infallible characteristics of forgery. On page 3 B we may note especially the tremulous *l* and *k* in the word "Almanak" (line 9), the mended *p* in "Cupids" (line 12), the patched *b*, *e*, and *l* in "Nobelmen" (in the margin),

the patched *e* in the absurdly altered "price" (in the margin), the shaky *l* in "Holiday" (line 18), the patched *K* in "Kings" (line 20 and in the margin opposite line 12), and the doctored *e* in "Reueng" (line 12).

How different the straightforwardness, directness, and forthrightness of genuine writing is from the weakness, vacillation, hesitancy, drawing, mending, and patching of forgery, is evident from a comparison of facsimiles 6 and 9.

That the writing on page 3 B was done with a kind of dye or paint, not with ink, and was painted over the letters that were originally traced with a pen or with a fine-pointed stylus, is shown in many spots—*e.g.*, the *g* in the word "Kings" (3 B 20), the *h* of "marche" in the same line, and in many of the Gothic letters, especially where, as Mr. Wood informs us, the paint has cracked off. See, for example, the *A* on page 5 B (eleventh line from the bottom of the page).

Further indications of forgery are to be found in the occasional omission of letters, because of the scribe's difficulty in seeing the finely outlined characters and because the heavily shaded letters took more space than the original outlines. Forgery is indicated also by certain errors which show that the writing (*i.e.*, the rewriting) was a mechanical process which took no cognizance of the calligraphic peculiarities of the script involved. Thus, for example, in 2 A 14 the word "Charges" lacks an *h*; in 2 A 17 the word "lodging" lacks the first *g*; in 2 A 19 "perticulars" is erroneously rendered "pertirulars" (the old *c* being mistaken for the twin-stemmed

Old English *r*); in 5A17 the word "Ossidewe" was bungled into something resembling "Ofssidewe" (and an attempt was made to conceal the tampering); in 5A19 the word "wier" shows that the word, as originally outlined, contained a *y* which was changed to a very poor *w* (the fine outline of the *y* is still visible); in 2B2 the down-stroke of the *g* (of the word "Chardges" in line 1) was drawn as if it were the whiplash of the *f* in the word "of"; in 6B13 in the word "allowance" the loops of the *l*'s were added subsequently to the writing of the bases of the letters; in 6B20 in the word "Imbassadors" (a word which also shows tampering with the last syllable) the remnants of a ghostly *I* are still clearly visible; the artificial stumps of the *l*'s are clearly shown in the *l*'s of "Allhollen" in 6B4; in 9A4 the word "ffiftene" was altered to "ffiftine," though to a Jacobean penman one was as correct a spelling as the other; in 7A9 "fower" was bunglingly altered to "four"; the two strokes, one straight and one curved, through the *a* above the word "Sum" in 8A28 (facsimile 7) tell their own story; a poorly concealed final *e* is apparent in the word "being" in 8A27; the abbreviating flourish above the *m* in "Sumer" (6B20) clearly shows a doubled outline; in 7B32 (facsimile 8) the outline for "w^ch" was mistaken for "w^th" (where the text clearly requires *which*); an impossible *a* appears above the word "William" in 8A12; and so forth.

The shading of the letters, when examined with a high-power lens (such as a Coddington 14), is seen to be brushwork, painting rather than writing. This is true not only of the heavily shaded Gothic letters but also of the Old English letters and the modern Roman letters. In fact, the writing everywhere is slow, labored, hesitant, and unnatural; only in a few lines does it suggest the ease, freedom, and naturalness of a writer accustomed to writing the script employed.

In the 1604-5 play-list (facsimile 3) the characteristics of forgery are no less apparent than in that of 1611-12 and in the rest of the documents. Here, too, we see spots where the dye or paint has cracked off, *e.g.*, in the *st* of "first" (3A1),[9] the *k* of "Banket" (3A2), the *r* of the second "Mesur" (3A8), etc.; the obscuring of the original outlines, *e.g.*, the top of the *T* in the word "The" (3A3); the persistence of final *e*'s which had not been properly inked over or sufficiently erased, *e.g.*, the *e* in "more" (3A11) and the bungled outline of the top of the *H* in "Henry" (4A7); the survival of original outlines which had not been painted in, *e.g.*, the terminal stroke of the *d* in "Cauled" (3A17); the omission of letters, *e.g.*, of a *c* in "Marthant" (4A15); the hesitancy and tremor of uncertainty and caution, *e.g.*, in the *K* of "Kings" (4A20); and other phenomena of the same kind.

There is no more convincing proof of forgery than the presence of changes and insufficiently erased outlines in matter that is of no consequence. Thus, for example, in 4A17 (facsimile 4*a*) the original outline was "Spainshe"; but when the forger went over his work he must have decided to omit the final *e*; fortunately, however, for the cause of historical truth, he did not succeed in erasing the outlined final *e*. The same phenomenon (the survival of an un-necessary final *e*) appears in the word "one" in 4A11. An even more striking instance of the persistence of an original outline, which the forger altered and forgot to erase, is to be seen in the word "Tragide" (4A16), which originally was "Tragidye." An Elizabethan or Jacobean penman would surely not have troubled to alter the spelling of his words, and he certainly would not if his spelling had been as freakish as that of the ostensible writer of these documents.

How untrustworthy and valueless a reduced half-tone facsimile of a questioned document may be is strikingly illustrated by Mr. Law's facsimile (*cf.* SSF, p. 17). In his facsimile of the word "Tragidye" no one would see that the letters *ye* are in ink of a different color and lie underneath what in his repro-duction looks like a blot or splotch of ink; in the word "one" (in the line "Euery one In his Umor") nobody would recognize the *e* as a survival of a pre-liminary sketch in ink of a different color; nor could one recognize the *e* in the word "Spainshe" as a survival of the original form of the word. Now, these three "ghosts," as I call them, are in themselves sufficient to damn these documents as forgeries! And yet Professor Dobbie, without examining this *ye* and these two *e*'s, reported that the ink was the same throughout! And Sir George Warner and Professor C. W. Wallace and others saw "absolutely nothing" to warrant a belief that these documents were forgeries!

We all occasionally retouch some-thing we have written. We do this either because we think the reader of the manuscript will have difficulty in readily deciphering the word, or because we see that the letter, as we committed it to paper, does not look like our pen-manship, *e.g.*, that an *e* looks like an *i*, an *l* like a *t*, an *e* like an *r*, and so forth. But we make these corrections in an offhand manner, with freedom and abandon, without any attempt at con-cealment or disguise. A forger, however, engaged in copying or imitating a model, attempts to mend and change the un-satisfactory letters in such a manner as to conceal the alteration; he tries to make the additional stroke or strokes join the others so that the joining will not attract attention. An amusing instance of patch-ing occurs in the bottom line of 6B, where the word "Horse" ("rent of his Horse") is changed to "House." Such delicately conducted repairs[10] in a writing —which are easily recognizable in en-larged photographs, especially if these are made by transmitted light—are con-clusive evidence of forgery.

Such telltale patchings and mendings occur in great numbers in both these Books of Accounts. In 8A13 (a bad line in many other respects) the final *e* in "like" (originally "leke"!) was given, wholly unnecessarily, an additional curl, which was tacked to the letter in a man-ner intended to escape observation (*cf.* facsimile 3). Such a superfluous piece of mending is conclusive evidence of fraud. The mending of the *5* at the end of 8A30, the last line, is extremely signifi-cant: the forger, seeing that this *5* was too much like his own *5*'s, conceived the idea of disguising it by putting an extra head on it and by putting an additional bit of shading to the bottom of the *5*. Both these bits of mending show up decisively in an enlarged photograph. Incidentally I may call attention to the peculiar and highly suggestive doubling of the *i*-dots in many parts of these documents. Striking instances occur in the words "this" (in the line containing the *5* we have just discussed), "*p*[ro]vitions" (in 8 A 29), and "Emptions" (in 8 A 28). Patchwork is also apparent in the *v* of "*v*ˢ" in 8 A 30. This *v* also shows clearly that at least two kinds of "ink" were employed in the manufacture of this document and that some of the letters were built up in sections. Curiously enough, the forger suffered from some defect of eyesight—astigmatism, in all probability—which betrayed him into placing his patches and alterations a trifle to one side of the strokes he intended to mend or cover up. This shows up vividly, in a photographic enlargement, in the tip of the final *s* in "years" in 8 A 30, in the tip of the *l* in "total" (8 A 28), and most conspicuously in the horizontal bars above the *T*'s (*cf.* facsimile 7).

It is also significant that there is in this document hardly a word that is written *currente calamo*; almost each letter was made separately and so joined to the preceding and succeeding letters as to give the impression of continuity. This is an infallible test of forgery. That the forger was not thoroughly familiar with the script he was copying is strikingly shown by an error visible in the word "Morover" in 8 A 24: he mistook the first *r* (the left-shouldered variety of the letter) for an epsilon-like *e*, and so we have a letter which is half

r and half *e*. In genuine writing such a thing is virtually impossible.

My distinguished predecessors in the investigation of these papers have taken it for granted that the signatures attached to these Books, on pages 8 A and 7 B, were beyond question genuine. The earlier Book bears what purport to be the signatures of "Ed: Tyllney," "Ed: Pakenham," "Wᵐ: Honyng," and "Edward kirkham." The later bears what purport to be the signatures of "G. Buc," "A. Stafford," "Wᵐ: Honyng," "Edward kirkham," and "Jo: Sotherton." All these signatures, I need hardly say now, are forgeries.

In the first place, it should be noted that such simply and legibly written signatures as those of Tyllney, Buc, Honyng, Pakenham, Kirkham, and Sotherton are easily imitated, as far as mere form is concerned, by anyone who takes the trouble to study them for a time, especially if he be a person with an aptitude for, and experience in, such work. Mr. William J. Lawrence called my attention to the fact that in Collier's manuscript *History of the Restoration Stage* (now preserved in the dramatic collection of the Widener Library at Harvard University, Cambridge, Mass.) the signatures of Charles Killigrew, Charles Hart, Nicholas Hart, Cardall Goodman, and Michael Mohun are needlessly imitated in the transcript of the complaint which these men made against Dryden."

In this connection I wish to call the reader's attention to a suggestive fact recorded by Richard Grant White in his edition of *The Confessions of William Henry Ireland* (New York, 1874, p. xxix).

He says: "Sir Thos. Duffus Hardy had in his possession a small sheet of paper on which were free—not traced—imitations of the handwriting of several of the persons connected with the Revels in the time of James I.; and these, it is quite certain, were made by Cunningham ... For this piece of paper is pasted in his own [*i.e.*, in Cunningham's] printed copy of the Revels Book [*i.e.*, the *Extracts*] which he edited; and this volume he himself gave [inadvertently] to ... Duffus Hardy." It is difficult to see how White could have been certain that Cunningham made the imitations.

In Edmund Tyllney's signature (8 A) there are several suspicious features: (1) The upstroke of the *d* looks as if it had been built up slowly and had been patched at the top. (2) The termination of the flourish is followed by a hair line which was not covered over with ink. (3) There is a colon after the *d*. In none of the Tyllney signatures that I have examined, *e.g.*, on page 1 of the text of *The Booke of Sir Thomas Moore* (1593?), in *MS. Lansd. 83, No. 63* (1598), in the Revels Accounts of 1587 (*A. O. 3/907*), in the Accounts for 1587-89 (*MS. Lansd. 59, No. 21*), etc., is there a period or a colon after the *d*. This colon is especially significant because we find it also in the alleged signatures of Honyng, of Pakenham, and of Sotherton; besides, as we have learned, the forger had a penchant for colons. (See facsimile 7.)

Such printed signatures as those of William Honyng, if we grant that he always printed his name, are perhaps the easiest to imitate.[12] I have, as yet, failed to locate even a single undoubtedly genuine signature of William Honyng. At the foot of the grant to Thomas Preston there is a signature of one "Honynges" that was written in 1564 and is in the Old English script, but it is almost certainly not the autograph of our Honyng. We must therefore judge the Honyng signatures in these Revels Accounts on their own merits. And, judged thus, they fail. It must be apparent to every eye that the writing is slow and hesitant; that the flourish connecting the first minim of the *W* with the overhead *m* is clumsy and artificial and not like what it would be in the script of a person accustomed to writing his name with such a device. This is also true of the mode of joining the *m* to the *H*. In both instances the attempt to conceal the joining is obvious. The ubiquitous colons, consisting of square-shaped periods, exactly as in 8 A 30, tell their own tale.

The signature of "G. Buc." in 7 B (facsimile 8) is a poor imitation—no doubt with some slight intentional variations—of the Master's signature in the licensing note in the manuscript (*B. M. MS. Lansdowne 807*) of *The Second Maydens Tragedy*. The square periods after and below the surname in 7 B, like those of the forger elsewhere, are in marked contrast to the round periods in Buc's memorandum.

The only other signature that I shall discuss here is that of John Sotherton, Baron of the Exchequer. His "signature" —"Jo: Sotherton: /:/."—occurs at the bottom of 7 B and is a fairly good imitation, so far as it is possible for the untrained eye to see, of John Sotherton's genuine signature in *Pipe Office Roll 2805*. But when the signature on 8 B is examined carefully, with a Coddington 14 lens, we discover indubitable evidences of forgery: The base of the first *t* was mended so as to bring this letter down to the level of the preceding *o*; the *h* was mended at the point where it turns to connect with the succeeding *e* (this was done to give this part of the *h* a sharp point, such as we have in the original); the *e* is not Sotherton's letter; the *o* before the *n* was mended (thickened) on the right side, was linked clumsily with the *n* (Sotherton's *o*'s seem not to have linked with succeeding letters), and was not made like Sotherton's *o*'s; the light strokes are heavier than in Sotherton's genuine writing; the line quality is not like Sotherton's. It is fairly evident, then, that this signature (on 7 B)

was built up in sections: the right half of the first *o* was an after-addition, as was also the head of the *e*. In Sotherton's genuine signature (*cf.* facsimile 8) the *h* linked with the adjoining *e* at the top of the letter, and the first minim of the *n* linked with the second by means of a looped upward stroke. Neither of these characteristics appears in the 1612 Revels signature.[13]

The study of the signatures, even so far as we have gone, corroborates the conclusions based on a study of the writing of the rest of the documents and confirms the conviction that, with the exception of the five bits previously discussed, these documents are forgeries from beginning to end. Their true nature should have been recognized long ago.

CHAPTER SIX

THE MALONE "SCRAP"

IN taking up the consideration of the Malone "scrap" we are entering upon the discussion of what has been supposed to be the most difficult and most perplexing phase of the whole subject.

Before the year 1880, when Halliwell-Phillipps published[1] his discovery of this small sheet of paper (measuring 7¼ x 8¾ inches) in a scrapbook (*Malone MS. 29*) at the Bodleian Library, the general verdict would unquestionably have been that the "Cunningham papers" were the clumsy handiwork of an amateur forger. But when the Malone "scrap" (*cf.* facsimile 10) was found to tally, "with almost microscopic accuracy," with the 1604-5 play-list, and to account for Malone's otherwise inexplicable knowledge of the dates of *Othello* and *The Tempest*, one of two conclusions seemed inescapable: (1) that this "scrap" had been in Malone's possession in or before 1800,[2] or (2) that he had had access to a Book of Accounts from which this imperfect and abridged transcript had been prepared.

Halliwell-Phillipps was so firmly convinced that the "Cunningham papers" were clumsy fabrications that he thought it impossible for so experienced an archivist as Malone to have been even temporarily deceived by the forgery

now in existence. And he was equally "sure" that Malone "would never have used the words 'indisputable evidence' ... until he had made a personal scrutiny of the originals." Halliwell-Phillipps therefore found himself compelled to assume "that the forger had met with, and [had] reproduced, in simulated form, trustworthy extracts from a genuine record that had disappeared from that [the Audit] Office."[3] From the late Dr. H. H. Furness we learn[4] that in reaching this conclusion Halliwell-Phillipps was swayed mainly by the notice in the play-list of a performance of *Love's Labour's Lost* which seemed to be verified by a letter from Sir Walter Cope to Cecil. This letter makes mention of a performance of this play by the King's Company in or shortly before January, 1605—a fact which, Halliwell-Phillipps thought, "could not have been known to the imposter."[5] Halliwell-Phillipps himself, we are informed by Dr. Furness, subsequently "acknowledged, in private correspondence, that the subject needed *entire* revision."[6]

Thus the matter stood until Mr. Law submitted the condemned documents for examination and obtained the verdict with which we are already familiar. That being so, the Malone "scrap" (with its peculiar spellings, etc.) and Malone's knowledge were seemingly explained, and there was no longer any mystery. To Mr. Law and to others, it now seemed clear that Sir William Musgrave, Commissioner for Auditing Public Accounts (1785-1800), had invited Malone, sometime in the last decade of the eighteenth century, to examine the Books of Accounts and Records of the Master of the Revels, which, in 1791, were still in the office for auditing the Public Accounts; that on Monday, December 2, 1799, he sent Malone "a Mem^dum about a MS which you have probably met with already—if not, it may furnish matter for some of your illustrations of Shakespear";[7] and that shortly thereafter, if not at the same time, he sent him an abstract of the 1604-5 play-list.

Mrs. Stopes ("Audi Alteram Partem"), as we have seen, refused to acknowledge the genuineness of the "Cunningham papers" or even the correctness of their data. She was therefore compelled to deny the authenticity of the "scrap." Fleay, we may point out, had taken very much the same attitude and on similar (though not identical) grounds. Mrs. Stopes argued that there was no positive evidence that Malone had been acquainted with the questioned Revels Accounts, had ever seen the "scrap," or had bequeathed the "scrap" to his posthumous editor, the younger Boswell. She made it quite clear, too, that there was not a particle of evidence to show that anyone had ever seen the "scrap" at the Bodleian Library prior to c. 1879, thus implying, of course, that the "scrap" was a forgery and had been "planted" among Malone's papers by someone who wished thus to vindicate both Peter Cunningham and the rejected Revels Books.

Realizing the importance of the "scrap," Mr. D. T. B. Wood made an independent examination of the matter and in consequence thereof made the suggestion that the "scrap" was "a deliberate plant by that 'Jekyll-Hyde' Payne Collier."[8] The following year, however, he announced[9] that as a result of further investigation he was convinced that Sir William Musgrave himself had written the pivotal "scrap." The facsimile of a two-page letter by Musgrave and of the "scrap" accompanying Mr. Wood's essay apparently settled the matter in the minds of almost all scholars. Those who, notwithstanding this, persisted in regarding the Accounts as forgeries were therefore driven to the theory that the Cunningham play-lists are copies of genuine papers, now lost, but they could not explain how this was possible if the paper on which the play-lists were written is an integral part of the Books containing them; nor could they offer any plausible explanation why anyone capable of such a forgery should have gone to all the trouble of executing it when the originals from which he worked were in existence. Is it any wonder, then, that today the Cunningham papers and the Malone "scrap" are still generally accepted as authentic documents of great literary importance?

In view of the material unfolded in the foregoing pages, I may very well be challenged to explain the Malone "scrap." To begin with, I might deny the relevance of the "scrap" to the real question at issue: whether the suspected Accounts are or are not genuine. But, realizing that issues of some importance are involved in the matter, I accept the challenge and confidently declare the Malone "scrap" to be a forgery, a studied imitation of Sir William Musgrave's penmanship, "planted" in the Bodleian Library by Collier where Halliwell-Phillipps might find it. The evidence for these conclusions—or, if you like, this verdict—is both direct and circumstantial, and may be marshaled thus:

1. In not a single one of Malone's publications—his *Shakespeare's Works*, published in 1790 and again in 1794; his *Historical Account of the English Stage* (1800); or his essay on *The Tempest* (1809)—is there the slightest hint as to the existence of any Revels Accounts other than those he reprinted in 1791. We may remind the reader that he closed his chapter on the Revels Accounts with the statement that no Revels records of the time of James I were known to be extant.

I shall, no doubt, be told, by way of rejoinder, that Malone's assertions concerning the dating of *Othello* and *The Tempest* and the production of *The Silver Age* show an acquaintance with the "scrap." But, as a matter of fact, they do not. For as regards *Othello* and *The Silver Age* his statements do *not* tally exactly either with the "scrap" or with the Revels Accounts; and *The Tempest* is not mentioned in the "scrap."¹⁰ Malone therefore probably acquired his information from other sources.

2. James Boswell, Jr., who edited Malone's *Shakespeare* in 1821, nowhere refers to the existence of any documentary evidence among the "Malone papers," entrusted to him in 1812 (the year of Malone's death), which would throw any light on the vexed questions we have been discussing. This clearly appears from a footnote (vol. 2, p. 404) to Malone's assertion that he knew that *Othello* was acted in 1604, he says: "Mr. Malone never expresses himself at random. I therefore lament deeply that I have not been able to discover upon what evidence he *knew* this important and decisive point." Boswell had evidently made a careful search. The importance of this fact is considerably heightened when it is remembered that Boswell had for years been a frequent visitor at Malone's house and would have been likely to hear something about these newly discovered Revels Accounts when Sir William Musgrave communicated them to Malone—had that really happened.

3. That a scholar like Malone, engaged in Shaksperian controversies with some of his best-equipped contemporaries, would have kept the knowledge of these Accounts to himself from 1791 (or even 1799) to 1812 is, to me, highly improbable.

4. Sir Edmund Chambers sums up thus one argument against the authenticity of the "scrap":¹¹ "It is inconceivable that, if the Jacobean as well as the Elizabethan books had then [in 1791] been discovered, no reference should have been made to them either by Musgrave or Malone, and the most probable explanation of the Bodleian scrap is that the Jacobean books turned up later, and that an abstract of the 1604-5 list was then prepared for the use of Malone. It is true that in that case the

Jacobean books would naturally have been added to the 'proper presses' which Musgrave says that he had provided for the Elizabethan ones, whereas Cunningham found the two sets apart. But," continues Sir Edmund, "as Cunningham also says that he had redeemed the Elizabethan bundle from 'a destructive oblivion,' it is possible that Musgrave's successors had been neglectful." That important official documents of the reigns of Elizabeth and James I, preserved in the Public Record Office and examined and transcribed by Malone and by Sir William Musgrave, and that only these, were so carelessly handled as to be rediscovered about 1838 "under the vaults of Somerset House ... in a dry and lofty cellar," I do not think probable. Besides, how can anyone say —assuming that he is trying to speak truthfully—that he has saved from a "*destructive* oblivion" papers which he, allegedly, found—among others, no doubt—in a "dry and lofty" cellar?

5. It is incredible that Malone would not have published the data in the "scrap" concerning the performance of *Measure for Measure*, or made certain that Boswell would do so. We must remember that but for this fact—if it be a fact that *Measure for Measure* was played at Court on December 26, 1604 —"nothing was known for certain about the history of this play."

And who that has the scholar's temper can believe that if Malone had known of the performance of *The Winter's Tale* by the King's Players on November 5, 1611, he would not have said so or would have been content with saying "I ... suppose [!] *The Winter's*

Tale to have been originally licensed by him [Sir George Buc] in the latter part of that year [1610] or the beginning of the next"?[12] To me this is *per se* almost sufficient to prove that Malone then had no knowledge of the Jacobean Accounts or of the "scrap."

Cunningham calls attention, in his notes,[13] to Malone's assertion that *The Comedy of Errors* "was not revived after the accession of the Scottish monarch." He points out, somewhat exultingly, that from these Accounts we know that the play "was not only revived, but revived, moreover, at Court." Again I say that it is incredible that Malone would have or could have kept the knowledge of such a fact to himself.

6. That the learned, persevering, and vindictive George Chalmers would have been ignorant in 1799—when he was publishing extracts from the Revels Accounts and from Herbert's Office-Book—of the 1604-5 and 1611-12 Revels Accounts, if such had been discovered by that time, is more than incredible. In his search for material with which to confound Malone and Steevens he left no stone unturned. That he was acquainted with the other Revels Accounts, we know. Considering that Sir William Musgrave had no intimate acquaintance with Edmund Malone (in his letter to him in 1799 he originally called him "Anthony"), we cannot believe that he would have hidden from Chalmers the discovery of two Books of Jacobean Accounts.

Some of the items in these Accounts fit in so well with some of Chalmers's theories[14] regarding the date of *Measure for Measure*, the revision of *Henry V*, etc., that it requires no great stretch of the imagination to picture what use he would have made of the new data in the exposure of Malone's ignorance and erroneous judgments. And, *per contra*, had Malone known of their existence, he would not have risked Chalmers's prior publication of them. The only plausible conclusion to be deduced from all this is that these Accounts (and, therefore, the "scrap") were not then in existence.

7. There is not a particle of evidence extant to show that the Malone "scrap" had been seen by anyone at the Bodleian Library or elsewhere prior to 1879. From Mr. Wood's letter (*loc. cit.*) we know that "not only Payne Collier, but Halliwell-Phillipps, who first found the *scrap*, were at the Bodleian together and working at the Malone MSS. in 1842"; and yet neither of them then discovered the "scrap"! I may add that Collier always had easy access to the Bodleian Library and was permitted to handle its books and manuscripts.

8. In his defense of the "scrap" against the attack of "Audi Alteram Partem," Mr. Law triumphantly says:[15] "That the 'scrap' was ... copied directly from the Record Office play-list ... — a hundred years ago — is pretty evident when we compare one with the other. For instance, in the play-list, line 5, the dot of the *i* in the word *Venis* happens to come just over the first portion of the letter *n*, ... and this peculiarity—due, doubtless, to hurried or careless writing—is curiously enough found to be followed in the 'scrap,' where the word is written as though it were meant to be 'Veins.' This fact scarcely supports the theory [of

Mrs. Stopes] that the two emanated from a common fraudulent hand, but suggests rather that the 'scrap' was the handiwork of a *scrupulous, but not very intelligent* copyist." (My italics.)

The objections to the above argument are many. Even if the "scrap" were an absolutely accurate and exact transcript of the play-list, it would not follow that it was made a hundred, and more, years ago.

If the contents of the "scrap" warrant the conclusion that the copyist was "not very intelligent" (*i.e.*, not intelligent enough to copy a fairly simple document accurately), then he could not have been Sir William Musgrave. That being so, what becomes of Mr. Wood's identification of Sir William as the penman?[16] Either Sir William did not write the "scrap" or it is not the work of a "not very intelligent [though scrupulous] copyist."

9. George Steevens, too, must not be lost sight of in this discussion. Nothing would have given that malicious and perverse scholar greater delight than to have caught Malone napping. Steevens had been a member of the Society of Antiquaries since 1767, and Sir William Musgrave would more than likely have told him something about the newly discovered Shaksperian documents. The absence of any reference to them in his writings is fairly conclusive evidence that they had no corporeal existence at the time.

10. The paper on which the "scrap" is written must now be considered. Mr. Wood tells us[17] that when he examined Sir Frederic Madden's correspondence at the British Museum, which contains

a number of letters by Payne Collier, he "was confronted almost immediately in 1839 by paper similar to that of the 'scrap.'"[18] He follows this up with the significant remark: "The *Malone MS. 29* [*i. e.*, the scrapbook in which the 'scrap' was found] came to the Bodleian in 1838." In his previous letter to *The Times* (*loc. cit.*) Mr. Wood had written as follows: "the Malone 'scrap' ... is written on paper which (in a large correspondence at the British Museum) occurs once between 1820 and 1830 and fifteen times between 1830 and 1844; and it [the 'scrap'] is not mentioned in the description of *Malone MS. 29* in the 1838 catalogue of Rodd, the bookseller, who sold it to the Bodleian in that year [?], though he mentions other curious Shakespearean memoranda in the volume." It is not superfluous in this connection to point out that Rodd himself was an enthusiastic, well-informed Shaksperian scholar who would have fully apprehended the significance of the "scrap."

On the third page of his essay on "The Revels Books" Mr. Wood has this very important remark: "The difficulty of the paper solved itself when the identical water-mark appeared on [blank ?] paper *adjacent to* one of Musgrave's letters" in the Audit Office. From this, presumably, Mr. Wood would have us infer that the paper is such as Musgrave might have employed. It seems not to have occurred to Mr. Wood that if a forger, *e.g.*, Collier, had gone to the Audit Office to make a study of Musgrave's penmanship for the purpose of imitating it, he might inadvertently have left a sheet of his paper among the Musgrave documents. How otherwise would the Record Office happen to preserve a blank sheet of paper bearing one watermark adjacent to a letter written on paper having another watermark?

11. Mr. Law, we have seen, thought the "scrap" the work of a scrupulous scribe. Had Sir William Musgrave made the transcript for Malone, it would undoubtedly—considering that he was himself an antiquary—have been made with the most scrupulous attention to every detail. Instead we find the transcriber guilty of serious and inexplicable departures from the original before him. He transposed the first two entries, thus putting them out of their chronological order; he omitted altogether the item about *The Spanish Maze* (see the discussion of this entry on page 22); he omitted the entry about a play having been "provided and discharged" on the Sunday following Candelmas Night; he omitted the item about *The Mask of Moors* given on Twelfth Night; he changed "Winsor" to "Windsor" (though he retained "Mesur"), "on" to "one," "Umor" to "humor," "Whit Hall" to "Whitehall," "Stivenes" to "Stephens," "Newers" to "New Years," "Labours" to "Labour," "Marthant" to "Marchant" (not "Merchant"), and "Foulles" (which he might have mistaken for "Fowls") to "Fools" (but retained "Boyes"). A scrupulous person would not have done these things. That Sir William Musgrave, an able antiquary, would have been guilty of such material alterations when he was preparing a transcript of a newly discovered official document for a noted scholar, is so improbable that,

per se, it almost convinces me that Musgrave did not write the "scrap." And yet there have been some who have marveled at the accuracy and fidelity of this transcript!

I think it suspicious, too, that the writer of the "scrap" knew enough to put the name "Ed^d Tylney" at the head of the sheet and to make "1604 & 1605" out of the erroneous and confused date at the head of 3A. Musgrave would hardly have done that. It was not necessary to tell Malone that in 1605 Tyllney was the Master of the Revels. Had Sir William written the "scrap," he would most probably have appended a description of the book as a whole and would have transcribed the names of all whose "signatures" appear on 7A.

Mr. Law's inference from the occurrence of the word "Veins" (for "Venis") in line 5 is, I think, negatived by the fact that in line 20 the scribe again wrote "Veins," though in the last entry in the play-list the word is "Venis," clearly enough. (*Cf.* facsimile 10.)

There are certain calligraphic features (*cf.* facsimile 10) in the Malone "scrap" which tell strongly against its genuineness. In line 2 the scribe began to write "Wifes" instead of "Wives"; in line 3 he bungled the word "Windsor"; in line 6 he wrote "Mesur by Mesur," and then corrected "by" to "for"; in line 17 the word "perf^d" and in line 19 the word "Every" show patchwork; in line 20 the scribe hesitated about writing "Veins" or "Venis" (though the writer of the play-list took extraordinary pains to write "V-e-n-i-s" in the "Shroutusday" entry), and the word "same" in the last line is obviously a bit of patchwork.

All in all, it seems as if *the scribe had not intended to make a faithful copy of the document before him, but had intended to introduce such departures from it as would suggest insufficient acquaintance with the matters dealt with therein.*

12. But, after all, the decisive question is whether the penmanship is or is not that of Sir William Musgrave. Mr. Wood, whose qualifications for the task are unknown to me, has apparently satisfied his readers that it is. That he erred in his identification can, I think, be shown beyond a doubt. Here follows Mr. Wood's statement of his case, as it appears in the first issue of *The Review of English Studies:*

"I was looking at the letters of Sir William Musgrave...when my attention was drawn to the marked similarity of two characteristics, the small *n*'s with a straight tail [*i. e.*, a horizontal terminal stroke] and the small *d*'s curved with a curl at the top (see facsimiles)...A close comparison of every letter with the hand in that immense accumulation made by Musgrave, the *Musgrave Obituary*, showed a fairly good agreement. Letters which differed at first sight were found to be written both ways; and two or three other marked characteristics appeared in both hands—the way in which the writer draws up final *a*, *e* and *r*. I was finally convinced by finding the rather curious *V* which occurs twice in 'Venice' in the *Scrap* ... The accompanying facsimiles show the general appearance of the two hands to be similar, and any one who makes a more critical examination will probably have little doubt that the hands are the same. It is hardly necessary for me to emphasise particular points, for practically every letter found in the *Scrap* can be paralleled in...Musgrave's writing: but special attention may be drawn to *B, E, G, H, K, L, Q*, and to the frequent use of dashes in place of stops."

In his second paper on the subject, Mr. Wood makes the following concession: "I was unfortunate perhaps in selecting for reproduction and comparison with the *Scrap* a carefully written official letter of Musgrave. There is in the facsimiles at first sight a certain *general dissimilarity in appearance*, as has been suggested by one or two experts; however exact is the similarity of forms of individual letters, it is better therefore to show a close general agreement with Musgrave's scribbled hand," as this hand appears in *Add. MSS. 5750-5756* at the British Museum.

It will be noted that Mr. Wood based his case wholly on two points: the *similarity in the forms of the letters* and the *frequent use of dashes in place of dots*. The latter is so obvious a feature in Musgrave's writing, and a characteristic so easily imitated, that it may be dismissed as of no value as a test of authenticity. Besides, Musgrave's dashes are firmer than those in the "scrap."

As to the *forms* of the letters, there are three replies to Mr. Wood: (1) The letters in the "scrap" are *not* identical with Musgrave's. (2) The horizontal final on the *n*'s, the little curl at the top of the *d*'s, and the wide-flung terminal stroke of final *a, r,* and *e*, are easily imitated and are very common features in handwriting of the period.[19] (3) The writing in the "scrap" differs

from Musgrave's in the far more important matters of *slant, speed, shading,* and *pen pressure*—the elements which are chiefly responsible for the "general appearance." Musgrave's genuine writing is heavier, less delicately shaded, and much more nearly vertical. Almost all the outstanding features in the "scrap" and in Musgrave's letters and penciled memoranda, *e.g.,* the capital *E*'s, the small *d*'s, the left-shouldered *r* without an initial upstroke, the pen-lifts after *w*'s, *v*'s, and *b*'s, the vertical, rodlike small *s*, the occasional horizontal ending-stroke of the words, the peculiar huddled combination between *i* and *n*, final *rs* resembling an *n* without a final upstroke, etc., are all characteristics of the writing of the period and have little personal identification value. Every one of these features may be duplicated in Collier manuscripts.[20] (*Cf.* facsimiles 11, 12, and 13.)

Inasmuch as Mr. Wood has singled out "the rather curious *V*" (there is really nothing "curious" about it) as the thing which convinced him that Musgrave (whom I shall herein designate as M) wrote the "scrap," I draw the reader's attention to the fact that M's *V* is not only a very simple letter, whose mere form is easily imitated, but that it differs from that of S (my designation for the writer of the "scrap") in one very important and probably significant feature, to wit, in lacking the little curl at the end of the final upstroke with which the *V* joins the succeeding letter. (*Cf.* facsimiles 11 and 12.) In my specimens of M's writing, this curl is always present; it is lacking in the two *V*'s in the "scrap" as well as in most of Collier's *V*'s.

Mr. Wood made special mention of the letters *B, E, G, H, K, L*, and *Q*. A study of facsimiles 11 and 12 will show that some of these letters, notably the *B, E, G*, and *L*, are identical—certainly as regards *form*—with the corresponding letters of Collier. They, therefore, prove nothing.

The two varieties of *H* (*cf.* facsimile 10) found in the "scrap" are extremely easy to imitate. And the *Q* and the *K* are so wholly unlike Musgrave's letters as to disprove—almost in themselves—the Musgrave attribution.

Musgrave's *Q* is a heavy, vertical, crabbed, ungraceful-looking letter. The *Q* in the "scrap" is a more or less elegant, markedly slanting, and rather graceful letter—and exactly like the *Q*'s made by Collier. (*Cf.* facsimile 15*a*.)

The only *K* in the Musgrave papers before me (there is none in the two-page letter facsimiled by Mr. Wood) is not like any one of the eight [!] *K*'s in the "scrap." (*Cf.* facsimile 10.) A mere glance reveals striking and significant differences between them. Collier's *K*'s resemble those in the "scrap" in every essential detail. (*Cf.* facsimile 14*a*.)

M's writing differs in several noteworthy features from S's. The former almost invariably fails to link a small *p* to a succeeding letter. In five pages of his writing, the *p* links with the letter following it only once. S links his *p* to the succeeding letter thirteen times out of sixteen! Besides this it must be noted that M's and S's *p*'s are very different-looking letters in shading, pen pressure, and form. M's capital *P* is also unlike S's in its minuter structure. (*Cf.* facsimiles 11 and 12.) Collier's *p*'s link with

the succeeding letter in almost every instance.

It is worth noting that when M writes proper nouns beginning with the sound of *j* he almost invariably employs a *J*. I have found only one exception to this rule (in a penciled memorandum of his in *Add. MS. 5753* in the word "Jno" [=John]). S, on the contrary, employs a capital *I* in both instances (in the word "January") in which we should expect a *J*. Though this is not an argument of much weight, it deserves to be presented.

The numerals in the "scrap" are much more like Collier's figures than Musgrave's. The quotation marks also are like Collier's rather than Musgrave's.

Such *of*'s, looking somewhat like tilted script *N*'s, as occur in the "scrap" in lines 2 and 10 occur nowhere in the M writings before me. The other instances of the word resemble those of Collier as much as those of Musgrave. (*Cf.* facsimile 15*a*.)

The laudable precision wherewith Musgrave indicated abbreviations and quotations in his letters is conspicuously absent from the "scrap." When M wrote "K" for "King" or "Q" for "Queen" or "Vol" for "Volume," etc., he was careful to put a period after the abbreviation; but not so S. (*Cf.* facsimiles 11 and 12.) It is surely significant that S is like Collier in his neglect of such details. Musgrave almost invariably indicates the beginning and the end of a quotation, but S does not.

In M the spacing between lines is remarkably uniform; but in S some lines are needlessly crowded together (*e.g.*, lines 8 and 9) whereas others are too far apart.

A striking point of difference between M and S is to be observed in the relationship of the writing to the left margin of the paper: The initial letters of M's lines form almost a perpendicular line close to the left margin; whereas a line drawn to join the initial letters of the successive lines in the "scrap" will make a zigzag line running markedly down and towards the right. In other words, S's left margin gets wider and wider as we go down the sheet; M's is practically uniform.[21] And it must be noted, too, in this connection, that M usually left almost no blank margin on the left side of the page he was writing on; S had a half-inch margin opposite the second line. The significance of such phenomena as these can be appreciated only by those who have studied many specimens of handwriting with the purpose of ascertaining those unconscious calligraphic habits of which the penman is not aware and from which he therefore never departs and is scarcely able to depart. (For a full and interesting exposition of this subject, see Mr. Albert S. Osborn's books, previously cited.)

To one who knows something of the personality of Musgrave and who is familiar with his pedantic exactness in writing, it is almost unthinkable that he would himself have written an abstract of one of the play-lists for a man with whom he was not personally acquainted, or that if he had done so,

he would have done it so incompletely, so inaccurately, and so slovenly. And a clerk, on the other hand, would surely not have dared to take such liberties with what he would have thought an important public document.

The above considerations compel me to conclude that the Malone "scrap" is a forgery. And when I consider the numerous indications of the hand of that tainted wether of the flock, John Payne Collier, I cannot help concluding that here scholars have another cause for grievance against him and another offense against the morals and ethics of scholarship to charge him with. That the fraud, notwithstanding its many defects, was done so well as to deceive scholars like Halliwell-Phillipps, Mr. Law, and Mr. Wood—an excellence which entitles this document to be designated Collier's masterpiece—makes the man's crime the greater.

It would not surprise me to meet with the objection to my condemnation of Collier that it is unbelievable for a forger to have imitated Musgrave's handwriting so well as to have deceived Mr. Wood and all others who had the opportunity to study the facsimiles (in *The Review of English Studies*, January, 1925). The objection is sufficiently answered, I think, by the reflection that some of Collier's interpolations in the Alleyn papers (at Dulwich College) were done so well that they escaped the scrutiny of the expert Sir George Warner (but not that of the much younger and more keensighted Dr. Greg).

CHAPTER SEVEN

COLLIER AND THE FORGED ACCOUNTS

AWARE of the seriousness of charging any man with having perpetrated and uttered a forgery, even a man so generally and justly condemned as perhaps the most mischievous (and most inexplicable) forger in the whole realm of letters, I shall herewith present evidence, both direct and circumstantial, which should leave not the slightest doubt, even in the minds of those most friendly to him, that the Revels Accounts of 1604-5 and 1611-12, as well as the Malone "scrap," were forged by John Payne Collier. From Mr. Law's book (SSF, p. 18) we have learned that when Mr. Bond, of the British Museum, asked Peter Cunningham to name a price for the documents he was offering for sale to that institution, the rum-soaked ex-clerk foolishly replied: "I have written to Collier about the Revels Accounts I sent you; and he will write to you." Collier, however, had more sense than to do anything so utterly ridiculous. And so we find Cunningham—as Mr. Law tells us—writing to Mr. Bond two days later: "I do not think that I am asking too much of the Trustees of the British Museum, when I ask Sixty Guineas for them." These items may fairly be construed as an indication that Cunningham thought or knew that Collier had a financial interest in the matter; though it *may* mean no more than that he thought Collier competent to set a value on them.

That Collier and Cunningham were active members of the same organization, the Shakespeare Society of London; were zealously searching for new matter bearing on the god of their idolatry; and were next-door neighbors, may be of significance in connection with our present inquiry. It is easily conceivable that a young man like Cunningham, overwhelmed by the attentions and flatteries of one of the most distinguished scholars of his day, might have succumbed to his persuasions and consented to participate in some of his forgeries—in the cause of what the older man would have been sure to say he knew to be the truth. But the more likely explanation, I think, is that he entered into Collier's plans as a "good joke" on the members of the Shakespeare Society. That he had guilty knowledge of the fraudulent character of the documents is proved by his deliberate omission of certain paragraphs from the transcript published in his *Extracts*.

Are there, it may not unreasonably be asked, any direct, tangible evidences of Collier's participation in the concoction of the Revels Accounts? In reply to this question it might be urged that the evidence of his hand in the Malone "scrap" constitutes a kind of direct evidence of his interest in these Accounts and therefore of his participation in their manufacture. But, fortunately, we do not have to rely solely on this line of proof. Examination of the manuscript discovers indubitable traces of his hand in the impugned documents.

It will be noticed that the suspected Accounts are written in three kinds of script:¹ (1) the bulk of the writing is the Old English "secretary" hand in general use for correspondence, accounts, etc., during the period to which these Accounts relate; (2) the names of the plays and the playwrights, as well as the companies, are in the Roman character which then was becoming more and more fashionable, especially for signatures, titles, and headings; and (3) certain words, e.g., the title, the names of the officials, and the opening words of paragraphs, are in black letter (Gothic). The first and third do not now concern us, but the second does.

It is a well-established principle in bibliotics that in the investigation of a questioned document only like writings should be compared, Roman with Roman, Gothic with Gothic, etc. The reasons for this are fairly obvious.

Collier, I need hardly say, wrote the Roman script. If, then, it is true, as bibliotists maintain, that a penman cannot conceal his unconscious writing habits, we ought to be able to detect some of Collier's personal calligraphic peculiarities in some of those bits of Roman script occurring here and there in the forged Revels Accounts. This we are able to do.

A study of facsimile 3 will show that the scribe's *L* (*e.g.*, in "Loues Labours Lost" in 3 A 19) is the same as Collier's in his unpublished *Emendations and Notes to Old Printed Plays*. This *L* occurs in almost all Collier manuscripts, genuine and forged, to which I have had access. (*Cf.* facsimiles 14 and 15.)

Minuscular *s*'s which resemble small huddled *5*'s, such as we see repeatedly in 3 B (*e.g.*, in the word "players" in the margin), also occur in Collier's *Emendations*. Such final *s*'s as we find in the word "Queens" in 3 B 14 and in "Ma^tis" in 3 A 18 are exact replicas of the final *s* in the *Emendations*, *e.g.*, in "MS" at the end of line 12 on p. 76 of volume 1. These letters all agree with one another not merely in form but in slant, proportions, and shading!

The Italic *h*'s in 3 B (*e.g.*, in the word "his" in the margin opposite the Gothic "Twelfe," line 13) show a curious tendency to the formation of a compound (concavo-convex) curvature in the vertical stem. This very *h* occurs fairly often in the pages of Collier's *Emendations*, *e.g.*, in the word "That" in line 8 of p. 76 in volume 1.

Collier's habit of beginning certain capital letters, *e.g.*, the *F* in "Fair" (line 18 of p. 95, *Emendations*), with a heavy horizontal stroke having a small downward hook at its beginning is one of the striking features in the play-lists, *e.g.*, the *V* in "Veins" (3 A 4), the *W* in "Wiues" and "Winsor" (3 A 6), the *P* in "Plaiers" (3 A 8), etc. How difficult it is for a forger to get away from his writing habits is nicely shown in the way Collier's *T*, in the word "Two" in his note on "*Two Noble Kinsmen*, A 1 sc 1 Dyce xi. 338, Wars or wear," recurs in the M [!] of "Marthant" [sic] in 4A15. It is undoubtedly a significant fact that Collier's T often constitutes the left half of his H's and W's.

Such small t's as we find in the play-lists, e.g., in the words "Ma^{tis}" (4A18), "Matie" (4A3), and "the" (2A12, 2A17, 4A20), are constantly met with in the *Emendations*, e.g., in the word "therefore" in line 20, p. 75, volume 2 (note on "*Two Noble Kinsmen* A1 sc 1"). It should be noted that these small t's are Collier's capital T minus the overhead horizontal element, e.g., in the word "The" in lines 3, 4, and 8 of page 75.

There are two characteristic letters in Collier's penmanship which are *per se* sufficient to identify him: They are his printed small r and his printed B. The former occurs in its most typical form in the words "Players" (3B18 margin, 3B19 margin), "Shaxberd" (3A7 and 3A12), and "Mesur" (3A8). In the *Emendations* this r occurs in lines 14 and 19 of p. 75, in the note to *Two Noble Kinsmen* A1 sc 1. (*Cf.* facsimiles 13*a* and 15.) The B, of which Collier gives us a single example in line 14 on p. 76, volume 1, in his note on *Dumb Knight*, occurs a number of times in both play-lists, most convincingly in "By" in 3B16, opposite the "Candelmas" entry. (*Cf.* facsimile 13*a*.) Incidentally it may be noticed how obvious is the forger's attempt to disguise these B's throughout the play-lists, especially in Book A. On the strength of this B alone no jury would, I am convinced, fail to convict Collier of being the fabricator of the play-lists and, therefore, of these Books of Accounts.

Access to other Collier manuscripts would in all probability reveal many other links connecting him with these forged Books.

Though it is unnecessary to adduce further evidence of Collier's guilt, I shall direct the reader's attention to significant matters of another kind. I shall do this not for the purpose of fortifying the case against Collier, though I may indirectly do so, but of demonstrating some interesting phenomena in the psychology of forgery and of confirming further my earlier opinion that these documents have not been studied so thoroughly and painstakingly as they deserved.

It is perhaps fair to say that—next to Professor Dobbie's report—Mr. Law's trump card (SSF, pp. 68-69) in the game of vindicating the "Cunningham papers" and Cunningham's character was the evidence of Sir George Warner, Keeper of Manuscripts at the British Museum, expert and specialist "in literary frauds and especially a specialist in Shakespearean forgeries. For it is he who, in his article on the life of John Payne Collier in *The Dictionary of National Biography*, and in his admirable catalogue of the Dulwich Manuscripts, has followed the forger over several of the most extensive fields of his fabrications, remorselessly tracking him letter by letter, and stroke by stroke, until the whole methods of the man's widespread and mischievous trickeries have been laid bare." Mr. Law goes on to tell us that "Sir George subjected the accounts . . . to a prolonged and searching scrutiny, and . . . was almost at once convinced that they were . . .

not the handiwork of Collier whose 'style' in forgery is only too well-known to him."

In rebuttal of Mr. Law's impressive argument, I call the reader's attention to a Collier forgery which Sir George has undoubtedly overlooked or ignored. In 1837—the date should be noted—Collier published his *Catalogue biblio-graphical and critical of early English literature in the library at Bridgewater House*, and in it (on page 41) he made the statement that he had before him a copy of Sir George Buc's *Daphnis Polustephanos* which the author had presented to Lord Ellesmere and which contained a signed "poetical inscription [six verses in Roman script] in Sir George Buck's handwriting." Fortunately for our discussion, a facsimile of the "poet-ical inscription" accompanies Collier's account. (This facsimile is reproduced in our facsimile 14*b*.) Examination of this facsimile shows, incidentally, (1) that, as is so often the case with forgeries and anonymous communications ("poi-son pen" letters), the poem is in a printed script; and (2) that the writer tried very hard to disguise his penmanship —hence the impossible *e* in the word "maner," uncrossed *f*'s in "Griffins," the impossible ampersand after the word "Great," the irregularities and inequal-ities in the spacing of the letters and words, the hesitancy in the formation of individual letters, the multiplicity of forms assigned to some letters (*e.g.*, the *w*'s and *r*'s), the extraordinary irregu-larities in alignment, the absurd little heads on *h*'s and *l*'s, the freakish *c* in "declare" (line 2), etc. That the penman-ship is not George Buc's is apparent at

a glance; that the inscription is a forgery is beyond the shadow of a doubt; that Collier was the forger may, in the light of what we know concerning him and his methods, be taken for granted.[2]

Let it be noticed how exactly the letter *g* in *Daphnis*, in the word "graue," reproduces the *g* in "Honyng" (near the bottom of page 7B) as well as the *g*'s in the words "Kings" (3B10 margin), "King" (3B7); the *g* of the word "great" (*Daphnis*, 4) reproduces the *g* in "Kings" (3B6 margin); the *g* of "obligations" (*Daphnis*, 4) reproduces the *g* of "Ring" (3B13 margin). These *g*'s occur also in Book A.

The small *r*'s in *Daphnis* are easily recognizable as the *r*'s of the Revels Accounts. Compare, for example, the *r* in "declare" (*Daphnis*, 2) with the *r* in "Larne" (3A15).

The most convincing evidences of identity between these two calligraphic specimens are to be found in the very remarkable *l*'s and *d*'s. Compare, for example, the *l* in "longed" (*Daphnis*, 1) with the *l* in "players" in 3B14 margin, the second *l* in "Thankfull" (*Daphnis*, 2) or the second *l* in "Gallant" (3B8). The *d*'s in *Daphnis, e.g.*, in "declare" (line 2) and "did" (line 5), are twin brothers to the *d* in 3B18 in the word "Holliday."

The *G*'s in "Great" (*Daphnis*, 1) and "Grissins" (line 6) are the product of the hand that wrote the *G* in "Gallant" (3B8).

Into the question of Collier's motives it is needless to enter in detail. In general it may, however, be said that most of his forgeries were probably intended to confirm his own guesses, conjectures, and surmises; that some were intended to substantiate such conjectures of others, *e.g.*, of Malone or of Chalmers, as appealed to him (we know that in the "Perkins Folio" he incorporated some of his predecessors' emendations); that still others were intended to confute the theories and conjectures of some of his predecessors and contemporaries. That he was a vicious and ill-natured controversialist we know from his biting comments on Dyce and others in his *Emendations*. That he was a little "cracked," if not actually demented, is clear from his propensity to concoct obscene and filthy poems and ballads which he pretended to have discovered, but of which no one had ever seen the originals.[3]

CHAPTER EIGHT

THE CAROLINE PLAY-LISTS

IN his *Extracts* (pp. xxiv-xxv) Peter Cunningham published for the first time a list of "Playes acted before the Kinge and Queene" in the "yeare of the lord. 1636," which he claimed to have discovered. Shortly after he had been compelled to return the Revels Books of 1604-5 and 1611-12 to the Master of the Rolls, it was found that he had disposed of this list to a London bookseller. Mr. Waller, the purchaser, hearing of the row about Cunningham and the recovered Books of Accounts, came forward and voluntarily surrendered the 1636-37 play-list.

After the publication of Mr. Law's first book, Mrs. Stopes vigorously attacked the authenticity of this play-list on historical as well as on calligraphic grounds. Mr. Law thereupon defended it, with perhaps undue vehemence, and made out what looked like a very good case indeed. Mr. Lawrence (*op. cit.*, p. 31) was convinced that "there [was] absolutely no reason for entertaining suspicion of the genuineness of this document"— an opinion which seems to be accepted generally.

Mr. Law expresses the opinion' that this play-list "seems to be in the handwriting of Eillaerdt Swanston." As to this identification of the penman, I can say positively that if any part of our "standard of comparison"—the Earl of Pembroke and Montgomery's warrant for payment to the King's Players in June, 1638—is in Swanston's handwriting, then Mr. Law is in error. Swanston's Old English script (*cf.* facsimile 17) is small, neat, graceful, fairly rapid, sharply defined, and artistic—the penmanship of an experienced and fluent penman. The penmanship of the play-list (*cf.* facsimile 16) is slow, deliberate, hesitant, coarse, blurry, and somewhat slovenly. The two specimens differ decidedly in the slant of the individual letters, the writing in the play-list being much more nearly vertical, and in the matters of alignment, shading, and pen pressure. Swanston's lines run straight across the page; those of the play-list follow a serpentine course across the page. In the former the writing presents a pleasing and rhythmical alternation of light and shaded strokes which is conspicuously wanting in the latter. The pen pressure with which the latter was written was much heavier than that of the former. The individual letters occurring in the two documents (the Pembroke-Montgomery warrant and the play-list) present such significant variations as cannot possibly have proceeded from one penman. Mr. Law was again too hasty in his identification.

That the writer of this play-list was attempting to imitate Swanston's penmanship seems to be fairly certain from a comparison of letters occurring in the list and in our standard of comparison. Note, for example, the capital E's in "Eyllaerdt" and "Easter," the word "of" in both documents, the small g's, the minuscular Italian h's, and the Old English p's. If the reader agrees with me that the penmanship of the play-list deliberately imitates Swanston's penmanship, he must, of course, reject the play-list as spurious.

But the spurious character of this document is established, wholly apart from the previous considerations, by the evidences of slowness, hesitation, patching, and mending. Such a patched and mended O as we have in the word "Oxford" (item 16) is practically inconceivable in the penmanship of a professional scribe. The head of the l in "Playes" (line 1) was obviously mended.[2] The deft doubling of the first minim of the u in "bush" (item 6) is pathognomonic of forgery.

The mending of the shading too is apparent throughout, e.g., at the bottom of the g in "Kinge" in line 1. That such phenomena are utterly inconsistent with the theory of genuineness goes without saying. In fact, the evidences of spuriousness are so conspicuous and so easily demonstrable that one wonders how they have escaped the attention of those who have hitherto studied the subject.

Although, so far as I can see at present, the matter has no direct bearing on the subject immediately engaging our interest, I must not omit to direct attention to some extraordinarily suspicious features in the Lord Chamberlain's Warrant of March 12, 1636-37 (*P. R., A. O. 3-908-No. 23*). This document, printed by Mr. Law (MASF, p. 71), directs Sir William Uvedale, the Treasurer of his Majesty's Chamber, to pay "John Lowen and Joseph Taylor, or either of them, for themselves and the rest of the Company of his Majesty's players," the sum of £240 for twenty-two performances[3] before his Majesty within the space of the year ended in February, 1636. Neither Mr. Law's comments nor his transcript gives the slightest hint that this document presents difficulties and evidences of having been tampered with. As a matter of fact, Mr. Law's garbled transcript is calculated to give the impression, to one who has not seen the original, that the document is quite all right.

Mr. Law says nothing, for example, of the fact that though Lowen and Taylor are named the payees in the warrant, the receipt is signed by Eyllaerdt Swanston, without a word being said regarding his authority to act for the company. And Mr. Law says nothing about the curious fact that the receipt is written in a hand which resembles closely, but is not, that of the penman who wrote the warrant. Nor does he call attention to the fact that Swanston alleges having received the sum of £240 on June 5, 1638, fifteen months after the date of the warrant, even though an endorsement on the back of the warrant says only that on a July 6 (the year is not specified) he received £100 on account. It is a fact that this endorsement (*cf.* facsimile 15*b*) presents us with two lines of writing acknowledging receipt of an additional £100; but these two lines are not in the handwriting of the person who wrote the words "Rec^d in ᵽte of this warr^t"; were evidently crowded in by a different hand; are in a "doctored" handwriting; and are worded in a manner which cannot be regarded as genuine. In an official document, acknowledging receipt of so much money, no one would merely crowd into a previous receipt the words "et more 20 decb^r 37—*l*^li" and doctor the *t* in "et" and make "20" out of what was originally the word "to"! And who will believe that in an official document of this nature the disbursement of another £50 would have been acknowledged merely by crowding in a line reading only "et more—*l*^li" and without mentioning the date? But this is not all. Mr. Law transcribes the endorsement in a manner implying that this was written in 1637; he omits the correct date—"1636"—and says nothing to show that another hand had bunglingly added the following items: "1637," "A1637," "1639," and "37" (after "July").

When Professor Joseph Q. Adams had read the preceding comments he suggested to me that, in view of the "striking and suspicious resemblances" between the play-lists of 1636-37 and of 1638-39, and notwithstanding his belief in the genuineness of the latter document, it might be worth while making a bibliotic examination of it. The present location of this play-list (*cf.* facsimile 18) not being ascertainable, I provided myself with a photostatic copy of the facsimile published, with a brief commentary by Mr. George Wright, in *The Journal of the British Archaeological Association* (December, 1860, vol. 16, pp. 275-76) and made a careful study of the writing with a high-power lens (a Coddington 14).

In his two-page essay, Mr. Wright gave no history of the document, but assured his readers of its undoubted authenticity. Students of dramatic history seem to be generally agreed that he "wholly misunderstood" the nature of the document he had brought to light. Notwithstanding Mr. Wright's confidence concerning the genuineness of the paper, "scholars have looked upon [it] with suspicion and apparently have treated it as a forgery" (J. Q. Adams, *Shakespearean Playhouses*, pp. 401-5).⁴ Mr. Lawrence joins Dr. Adams in regarding the document as genuine.

This bill consists of a single sheet of paper measuring approximately 9 x 7 inches and is slightly torn all along the right and left margins, less along the left than the right. The lower margin was evidently cut away with a knife. A fragment, measuring *c.* 1 x 2 inches, is missing from the upper left corner. There is a vertical crease along the middle of the sheet. The writing is the Old English "secretary." In the upper right-hand corner someone subtracted "1638" from "1793" (originally "1792"), leaving "155." Regarding the composition of the ink, the quality of the paper, and the watermark, I am in no position to say anything.

That the document is a bold forgery admits, in my mind, of no doubt, even though to the naked eye it presents no very suspicious features. When it is examined microscopically, it shows the familiar characteristics of a forgery by an individual who did not even think it necessary to master the alphabet of the script he was attempting to imitate. There is hardly a letter in the thirty-two lines of this document that has been made correctly or naturally. Almost every letter has been mended, corrected, or patched; little bits of shading have been added here and there. The forger's uncertainty as to the forms of the letters and the mode of joining them betrays itself in the presence of unnecessary minims (*e.g.*, between the *c* and the *p* in "Cocpit" in the entries for November 8, 15, 22, etc.). The *sh* in "The Spanish Caratt" (January 7), the *R* in "Richmount" (January 1), the *th* in the first "the" in the December 18 entry, the *cp* in "Cocpit" (May 31), the *C* in "Coopit" [*sic*] (November 8), the *ost* in "Costome" (November 27), are enough to condemn this document as being a gross and poorly executed forgery. Unusual, abnormal tremors and pauses at unnatural points in the writing occur in great abundance. In fact, there is not a clean-cut pen stroke anywhere in the document. The list was evidently painted, not written.

From a bibliotic viewpoint one of the most curious features about this list is the forger's evident desire to disguise his *8*'s. When they are examined with a lens, these *8*'s disclose evidences of patching and mending, as well as a very suspicious horizontal crossbar at the top; not a single one of these *8*'s (of which we have four, not counting the one in the upper right corner) was written *currente calamo*.

Though the expert bibliotist usually conducts his investigation without any regard to such external circumstances as the history of the document, the issues involved, the character of the owner, and so forth, the layman's (the juror's) judgment is very often much more impressed by some striking fact in the provenience of a questioned paper. I have therefore investigated the history of this play-list and have learned[5] that Mr. Wright represented it as having been a leaf from a theatrical manager's book and as having been found (he did not say by whom, how, or when) in a manuscript volume which he exhibited and which was lettered *Notitia Dramatica*. This volume, he informed his audience, contained "scraps and memoranda collected by the celebrated Isaac Reed, *from 1734 to the close of the century*. On the reverse of the leaf was written, 'This old play-bill was in the papers late the property of Sir W. Foredice' (Sir W. Foredice, a well-known physician, who died in 1792)."[6] Mr. Wright, I may add, referred to Cunningham's *Extracts* in the course of his remarks, thus indicating some knowledge of the subject.

Realizing that if this document came from Isaac Reed's collection it could not be a nineteenth-century forgery, I turned to the 1807 sales catalogue of Reed's library, and found there the following interesting item (Lot 8833, on p. 399):

"*Notitia Dramatica*, both printed and manuscript. Containing a Chronological Account of the chief incidents relating to the English Theatres, from Nov. 1734 to 31st Dec. 1785. Collected from various sources, but chiefly the Public Advertizers which were lent me by Mr. Woodfall, for the purpose.

"This volume contains the most material facts relating to the Theatres *for the last fifty years*, and will be useful to any person who may wish to compile a History of the Stage.

"Isaac Reed, Staple's Inn, August 6, 1784."

A perusal of the above will convince anyone, I think, that the play-list under discussion, dated "1639," did not come from Reed's *Notitia Dramatica*. Having his eye on a "History of the Stage," Reed would hardly have included an important early seventeenth-century document in a book devoted to the second half of the eighteenth century. I have very little doubt, therefore, that Mr. Wright was the victim of a deception.[7]

It has been suggested to me that Reed, painstaking and accurate scholar though he was, might have inserted this play-list into his book of memoranda to preserve it; but I do not think this probable in view of the fact that Reed, as Lot 8713 in his catalogue instructs us, kept a special book for general *Theatrical Memoranda*. His *Notitia Dramatica* was restricted to the years 1734 to 1785.

APPENDIX A

PROFESSOR DOBBIE'S REPORT

Government Laboratory,
    Clement's Inn Passage,
    Strand, London, W.C.

        6th December, 1910

Sir,

In accordance with the request contained in your letter of the 23rd November last, an examination has been made of the ink used in writing an Account Book of Revels in the year 1604-5, now preserved in the Public Record Office.

The document was brought to this Laboratory by Mr. Stamp of your Department in whose presence the whole of the examination was carried out.[1]

The book contains six leaves. The first leaf, forming pages 1 and 2, was loose, and had apparently been torn from the last leaf (pages 11 and 12). The second leaf, forming pages three and four, is part of the same sheet of paper as the fifth leaf (pages 9 and 10). The two central leaves, forming pages 5, 6, 7, and 8, are in one sheet.

Mr. Stamp stated that the special object of the enquiry was to ascertain whether there is evidence that the ink on pages 3 and 4 is of different character or of different age from the ink in other portions of the document.

The entries on pages 3 and 4 are apparently complete in themselves, and many of the words are in the Italian hand. For example, the titles of the plays, and the names of the authors and the companies of actors, are consistently in that form of writing. It should, however, be noted that the Italian hand also occurs on page 2 in the words "Jacobi", "ano" and "anno"; and on page 1 and page 8 in the word "ano".

There are several alterations on pages 3 and 4. "1605" at the head of page 3 has been altered to "1604"; the word "Names" in the margin of page 3 has been crossed out with transverse lines; the letter "e" has been added to the words "on" and "Spanisch" on page 4; and the letters "ye" have been written over the final letter "e" of "tragide" on page 4. The ink used in making these alterations does not appear to be different in character from that on the other pages.

Excluding the signatures on pages 8 and 9, the general appearance of the ink throughout the whole book, inclusive of pages 3 and 4, is similar. There is no indication that the ink in one portion has faded more than the ink in another portion. If pages 3 and 4 were written, in or about 1868[2] as suggested, to match the other writing of the document, at that time 260 years old, I should have expected to find that the 1868 writing had faded during the past forty years to such an extent as no longer to resemble exactly the older writing which probably has undergone little or no change since 1868.

When examined microscopically, the ink presents similar characteristics throughout the whole document. It has consistently the same glistening gummy appearance; and in drying has frequently shrunk from the paper, forming fissures and cracks through which the unstained fibre of the paper may be seen. No difference is discernible in any of these respects between the ink on pages 3 and 4, and that in other parts of the document. With one exception, a different ink has been used for the signatures.[3]

The ink has not penetrated into the paper fibre to a greater extent on pages 3 and 4 than on the other pages. It was therefore most probably of the same degree of fluidity, and the paper at the time of writing of the same surface and condition.

The ink has also been examined chemically. Portions of the writing on pages 3 and 4 were treated with chemical reagents and the effects produced compared with the action of the same reagents upon marks of similar density selected from the writing on page 2.

The chemical examination gave no indication of any difference, either in the constituents of the ink or in the degree of resistance to bleaching agents, between the ink on pages 3 and 4, and that in other portions of the document examined.

A consideration of all the observations made in the course of the examination leads to the conclusion that the ink used is of the same character throughout the document.

There is no evidence in my opinion to support the suggestion that the writing on pages 3 and 4 is of a different date from the writing on the remainder of the document.

I am, Sir

Your obedient Servant,

(Signed) James J. Dobbie

The Deputy Keeper of the Records,
Public Records Office,
Chancery Lane,
London.

———

Letters or portions of letters in the document which have been treated with chemicals.

On Page 2

Letter   above letter "h" in 1st "the".

Mark   above letter "h" in 1st "the".
Mark   above letter "h" in 2d "the".
Mark   above letter "f" in "of".

On Page 3

Mark   above "Hallowmas".

Letter   in the margin.

On Page 4

Letter   in "on the 7".

Mark   above "h" of "night".

Mark   above "f" of "twelfe".

Letter

APPENDIX B

THE VERTUE MANUSCRIPT[1]

[47ʳ]

Itm̃ paid to Joseph Taylor vppon the Cowncells warr'[2] dated att Whitehall xxviijᵒ Die Junij 1613 for him self and the rest of his Company the La: Elizabeth her graces servanntes and players for presentinge before the Princes Highnes, Cownte Pallatyne Elector, and the La: Elizabeth two severall playes viz one playe called Cockle de Moye,[3] on the xxvᵗʰ of ffebr: last and one other called Raymond Duke of Lyons[4] on the first of March followinge the some of

xiijˡⁱ vjˢ viijᵈ./—

Itm̃ paid to Germane Marsham vppon a warr' signed by the Lo: Chamberleyne and Mʳ Channcellor dated att Whitehall xviij Die Septem̃: 1613 for his Charges and paynes in bringinge Leг̃es[5] for his Maᵗˢ service from Bruxells the some of

xˡⁱ./—

Itm̃ paid to William Joanes vppon a Warr': signed by the Lo: Chamberleyne and Mʳ Channcellor dated att whitehall xxvjᵗᵒ: Die Julij 1613 for his Charges and paynes in bringinge Leг̃es for his Maᵗˢ service from Parris the some of

xvˡⁱ./—

ᵽet Cowncells Warr'[6]   [47ʳ]

Itm̃ paid to Gilbert Diglen vppon the lyke warr' dated att whitehall xviijᵒ Die Septem̃ 1613 for his Charges and paynes in bringinge Leг̃es for his Maᵗˢ Leг̃es for his Maᵗˢ service from Copen Haven the some of

xvˡⁱ./—

Itm̃ paid to Thomas Sympson one of the Messengers of his Maᵗˢ Chamber, vppon the Cowncells warr' dated att Whitehall vltimo Die Julij 1613 for money layed owt by him aswell for horsshyer Dyett and Lodginge of one Phillipp Shawe whome he brought owt of the Cowntie of yorke vnto Whitehall and kepte him in his Charge the space of xxxᵗⁱᵉ dayes, the some of

xˡⁱ xjˢ—

Itm̃ paid to John Heminges vppon lyke warr': dated att Whitehall ixᵒ Die Julij 1613 for himself and the rest of his fellowes his Maᵗˢ servanntes and Players for presentinge a playe before the Duke of Savoyes Embassadour on the viijᵗʰ daye of June 1613 called Cardenna[7] the some of

vjˡⁱ xiijˢ iiijᵈ

70-11-0 exʳ

[47ᵛ]

Itm̃ paid to John Heminges vppon the Cowncells warr' dated att Whitehall xxᵒ Die Maij 1613 for presentinge before the Princes Highnes the La: Elizabeth and the Prince Pallatyne Elector fowerteene severall playes viz one playe called ffilaster, One other called the knott: of ffooles,⁸ One other Much adoe abowte nothinge, The Mayeds Tragedy, The merye Dyvell of Edmonton, The Tempest, A kinge and no kinge. / The Twins Tragedie⁹ / The Winters Tale, Sᵣ John ffalstafe, The Moore of Venice, The Nobleman,¹⁰ Caesars Tragedye.¹¹ / And one other called Love Lyes a bleedinge, All wᶜʰ Playes . weare played wᵗʰⁱⁿ the tyme of this Accompte, viz pᵈ the some of   ˣˣ
                    iiijxiijˡⁱ vjˢ viijᵈ . / —

Itm̃ paid to the said John Heminges vppon the lyke warr': dated att Whitehall xxᵒ die Maij 1613 for presentinge sixe severall playes viz one playe called a badd begininge [sic] makes a good endinge,¹² One other called yᵉ Capteyne,¹³ One other the Alcumist. / One other Cardenno. / One other The Hotspurr.¹⁴ / And one other called Bene-

dicte and Betteris¹⁵ All played wᵗʰⁱⁿ the tyme of this Accompte viz pᵈ — ffortie powndes, And by waye of his Maᵗˢ rewarde twentie powndes In all
                    lxˡⁱ . / —

ᵱet Cowncells Warr ¹⁶

Itm̃ paid to Phillipp Rosseter vppon the Cowncells warr' dated att Whitehall xxiiijᵗᵒ Die Novembris 1612 for himself and the Children of the Queenes Maᵗˢ: Revells, for presentinge before the Princes highnes: the La: Eliz : grace, and the Cownt Pallatyne, a Com̃edye called the Coxcombe¹⁷ the some of

                    vjˡⁱ xiijˢ iiijᵈ —

Itm̃ paid to the said Phillipp Rosseter vppon the lyke warr': dated att Whitehall vltimo die Maij 1613 for presentinge two severall playes, before the Princes highnes, One vppon the ixth of Janu'ie last called Cupides revenge,¹⁷ And the other called the Widdowes Teares,¹⁸ vppon the xxvijᵗʰ of ffebr: followinge the some of
                    xiijˡⁱ vjˢ viijᵈ —

                    173-6-8 exᵣ

APPENDIX C

TRANSCRIPT OF PLAY-LIST A

The pla= iers [names]²	; 160[4]5 ;¹	The poets
	Hallamas Day being the first of: Nouembar A Play in the Banketinge: house att Whit Hall Called *The Morr³ of~ Veins*:	*wᶜh mayd the Plaies ~ ~.*
By the Kings Maᵗⁱˢ Plaiers:.		
By his Maᵗⁱˢ Plaiers~.	**The Sunday** ffollowinge Aplay of the Merry Wiues of Winsor: .	
By his Maᵗⁱˢ Plaiers:.	**On; Sᵗ; Stiuens night** in the Hall A play Caled *Mesur for Mesur*:	*Shaxberd:*
	On Sᵗ Jhons⁴ night A **maske** wᵗʰ Musike presented by the Erl of *Penbrok* the Lord Willowbie &: 6: kinghts mor[e]⁵ of yᵉ Court	
By his Maᵗⁱˢ Plaiers:.	**On Jnosents Night** The plaie of: *Errors*	*Shaxberd:*
By the Queens Maᵗⁱˢ Plaiers:	**On ; Sunday ffollowinge** Aplaie Caled *How to Larne of a woman to wooe*	*Hewood*
The Boyes of= the Chapell:.	**On Newers Night** A playe Cauled : *All Foulles* :	*By Georg Chapman*
By his Maᵗⁱˢ Plaiers:.	**Betwin Newers Day** And Twelfe Day Aplay of *Loues Labours Lost*:	

[P. 4]

The plaiers[6]		The poets
	On Twelfe Night The Queens[7] Ma^{tis} Maske of Moures wth Aleven Laydies of Honno^r to Accupayney her ma^{tie} wch cam in great showes of devises wch thay satt In wth exselent Musike	
By his Ma^{tis} Plaiers:	On the ; 7 ; of January was played the play of *Henry the fifth:*	
By his Ma^{tis} Plaiers: .	The ; 8 ; of January; A play Cauled *Euery on out of his Umor*	
By his Ma^{tis} Plaiers: .	On Candelmas Night A playe *Euery on[e][8] In his Umor*	
	The Sunday ffollowing A playe provided And discharged	
By his Ma^{tis} Plaiers:	On Shrousunday A play of the *Marthant of Veins*	*Shaxberd*
By his Ma^{tis} Plaiers: .	On Shroumonday A *Tragid[ye]e[9]* of The *Spainsh[e] Maz:*	10
By his Ma^{tis} Plaiers: .	On Shroutusday A play Cauled *The Martchant of Venis* Againe Cõmanded By the *Kings Matie*	*Shaxberd:*

APPENDIX D

TRANSCRIPT OF PLAY-LIST B

The, names, of the Playes And by what Cumpaney Played[1] them Hearafter ffollowethe : As Allso what Maskes, and Triumphes[2] att the Tilte woere presented[e][3] before the king*es* Matie in this year. / 1612.

By the Kings Players : Hallomas; Nyght was presented att Whithall before ye king*es* Matie

A Play Called the *Tempest :*

The Kings Players : The: 5th: of, nouember: A Play Called[3] ye winters Night*es* Tayle /
The Kings Players :

On : S^t; stiuenes Night A play called A King & no king, & Rũing at ye Ring[4]

The Queens players : S^t; John; Night A Play Called the *City Gallant.*

The princes players : The; Sunday, ffollowinge A Play called the *Almanak*

The Kings Players : On neweres, Night A Play Called the *Twiñes Tragedie/* And Ruing att the Ring.

The Childern of whitfrie[a]rs The Sunday ffollowing A Play Called *Cupids Reueng*

This day the King & prince, Twelfe, Night The *Princes Mask performed by Gentelmen*
wth diuer of his Nob[e]ilmen[5]
did rũn att y^e Ring for of his Hid[6]
a pri[c]ze.[7] /

By the Queens players The; sunday: ffollowinge att Grinwidg before the Queen and
and the Kings men the Prinee[8] was Playd *The Siluer Aiedg :* and y^e next Night following *Lucr̃c*

By the Queens Players = Candelmas: Night A Play Called *Tu Coque /*
By the Kings Players S[t]broue[9]; Sunday: A *Play Called the Noblman*

By the Duck of Yorks Shroue; Munday: A Play *Called Himens H[a]oliday[10]*
Players /
By the Laydye Elizabeths Shroue; Teuesday A *Play Called the proud Mayds Tragedie*
Players /

On the 24^ty: day of marche Being the *Kings Ma^tis* Day of his Entrie to the Croune of England was performed at ye Tilt A Triumphe

CUNNINGHAM'S OMISSIONS

The paragraphs omitted by Cunningham in his transcript of the Accounts of 1604-5 and 1611-12 are so important for our study that I transcribe them here:

1. **Edmundo Tylney** Ar' Maḡro Revellor' per
ipm̄ exponend' vers' exoneracōnem oueru' Cresceutiu' in eo Officio pro hoc anno prefait'. 1605. per
brē sub privato sigillo dormiens dat' xxj^mo die decembris. 1604 Anno regni sui Anglie ffrancie et ~
Hibernie Sc̄do et Scotie xxxviij^no C : ^li

These six lines constitute the second paragraph from the bottom of page 2A and are enclosed within braces. They allege that £100 were advanced to Edmund Tyllney to enable him to discharge the duties of his office in the year 1605 and that the advance was made on the authority of a warrant dormant ("privato sigillo dormiens") dated December 21, 1604. The name of the reigning monarch is conspicuously absent, although it is clear that James I was meant. At this time Sir George Buc was Acting Master of the Revels.

2. On the left side of the omitted paragraph, opposite the lower half of the enclosing brace, occur the following words (five lines):

derrar p'stit' | extra Recept' |
Saiȷ^a procausis | Jnfra script' : |
Viz:

These words mean: "Money [is] guaranteed beyond the receipt of the exchequer for items mentioned below." The writing is very bad. The first word is clearly "derrar," though it should be "denarij." The abbreviation "Saiȷ^a" for "Saccarij" seems to be unique.

3. Below the preceding paragraph occur these five lines, which were also omitted by Cunningham:

But ther was payed in the sayd terme of S^t
Michaell vnto ye sayd M^r of the Revelles ye som̄e
of Threscore six pound*es* nyne shillinges ten pence
being the S^rplusage of his Accompt for the
year ended the last of October : 1604 :

It would be interesting to know why Cunningham omitted these lines and what he thought they meant.

> The: mr | of ye Revell*es* | demands |
> & other ye | Officers & | Attendāces |
> of ye Servis | as it hathe | bin hertofore |
> allowed: ye Mr | att iiijs the | Officer att |
> ijs the rest | att xxd & xijd: | the day and |
> as mouche | by Night — | A pece.

This may have been omitted inadvertently.

5. At the top of page 9 A is an important paragraph, in the forged

4. In the margin of page 7 A appear the following eighteen lines, which Cunningham omitted:

handwriting, which Cunningham did not print in his *Extracts* (p. 209). It should be compared with omission 1. It reads:

> More the said Mr of the Revell*es* demandeth Allowaunce
> for the Srplusage of his last Accompte in the foote⁓
> therof Appeareth being before chardges the Some of ⁓
> Threscore ffift[e]ine pound*es* ffive Shilling*es* tow pence: .
>
> Ed Tyllney
> xixno Decembris 1605

6. Just below the preceding item there occurs the following affidavit in

the manuscript, but not in the *Extracts*:

> Edmundus Tylney Ar Magister de lez Revell*es* prestitit sacrũ
> dčis die et anno coram me. *Tho: fflemyng.*

In none of the other Accounts is there such an affidavit. What oath the Master took, the document does not say.

For Cunningham's other omissions, the reader is referred to the discussion on page 29.

APPENDIX F

WRIGHT'S PLAY-LIST

before the king & queene this   1792 [3]
yeare of our lord 1638   1638
                                     _____
                                       155

At the Cocpit the 26th of march   .   .   .   .   The lost ladie
At the Cocpit the 27th of march   .   .   .   .   Damboyes
At the Cocpit the 3d of Aprill   .   .   .   .   Aglaura
At the blackfryers the 23 of Aprill for the queene the vnfortunate lou
At the Cocpit the 29th of may the princes berthnight   ould Castel
At the Cocpit the last of may agayne the   .   .   vnfortunate louer
At Sumerset=house the 10th of July & our day
— lost at our house mr Carlels play the first part of the pasionate louer
— At hamton Court the 30th of September   .   .   The vnfortunate loue
— At Richmount the 6th of november for the ladie[s]   ⎫
  maries berthnight & the Day lost at our house   ⎬ The mery Duell [!] of Edmonto
— At the Cocpit the 8th of novembe   .   .   The fox
At the Cocpit the 13th of november   .   .   .   Ceaser
At the Cocpit the 15th of november   .   :   .   The mery wifes of wins
At the Cocpit the 20th of november   .   .   .   The fayre favorett
At the Coccpit [!] the 22th of november   .   .   .   Chances
At the Coopit the 27th of november   .   .   .   The Costume of the C
At the Cocpit the 29th of november   .   .   .   The northen las
At the Cocpit the 6th of Desember   .   .   .   The spanish Curatt
At the Cocpit the 11th of Desember agayne   .   .   The fayre favorett
At the Cocpit the 18th of Desember in Carlels
  play agayne the first [?] part of   .   .   .   .   The pasionate louer
At the Cocpit the 20th of Desember the 2d part of   The pasionate louer
At the Cocpit the 27 of Desember the 2d part agayne of the pasionate louer
— At Richmount the 28 of Desember The ladie   ⎫
  Elsabeths berthnight & our day lost at our house   ⎬ The northen las
— At Richmount on newyeares Day   ⎫
  and our Day lost at our house   ⎬   .   .   beggers bush
— At Richmount the 7th of Janeuarye   ⎫
  and our Day lost at our house   ⎬   .   .   The spanish Cara[tt]

NOTES

NOTES

PREFATORY NOTE

PAGE viii

¹ In my *Booke of Sir Thomas Moore: a Bibliotic Study* (1927) I defined the term *bibliotics* as "the science which studies the characteristics of a document for the purpose of determining its genuineness and of establishing the identity of the person who wrote it."

CHAPTER I

PAGE 1

¹ The Revels Books are the official account books of the Master of the Revels, whose business and duty it was to prepare masques, shows, and plays for the entertainment of the King at Court. The Master's official year, in the reigns of Elizabeth and James I, began on November 1 and ended the following October 30. His accounts, presented annually to the Treasurer of the Chamber for payment, carefully and minutely set forth all expenses incurred by him and his subordinates in the preparation of the grounds, buildings, halls, costumes, etc., required for the performances before the reigning sovereign.

² *Extracts from the Accounts of the Revels at Court in the Reigns of Queen Elizabeth and King James I . . With an Introduction and Notes by Peter Cunningham.* London, 1842.

³ In his book, *Supposed Shakespeare Forgeries* (hereafter referred to as SSF), 1911, p. 33, Mr. Ernest Law asserts emphatically that Cunningham "did not go to the Museum" when he offered the documents for sale. Though the point is really of no consequence, it is perhaps worth noting that in the London *Times Literary Supplement* (February 10, 1921, p. 91) Sir Edward Maunde Thompson says that he was working at the British Museum with Mr. E. A. Bond "when Mr. Cunningham called on Mr. Bond in connexion with his offer." Mr. Law's statements must be accepted with caution and his quotations need checking.

PAGE 2

⁴ Quoted from Mr. Law's SSF, pp. 41–42, to which book the reader is referred for a vividly detailed account of some of the historical matters dealt with in this chapter.

PAGE 3

⁵ I may perhaps be permitted to say here that in my review of Mr. Law's first book I expressed myself as not wholly satisfied with the case he had made out on paleographic grounds, and pointed out what I considered essential weaknesses in his arguments. See *The Dial*, Chicago, July 1, 1914, vol. 57, pp. 16–17.

⁶ Preceding the publication of her little book, Mrs. Stopes had contributed two letters on the subject to December 2, 1920 (p. 798), and on February 24, 1921 (pp. 127–28). Mr. Law defended the documents in the same journal on December 23, 1920 (p. 876); December 30, 1920 (p. 891); and January 27, 1921 (pp. 59–60).

⁷ "Was Peter Cunningham a Forger?" *Modern Language Review*, January, 1924, vol. 19, pp. 25–34.

PAGE 4

⁸ "The Revels Books: the Writer of the Malone Scrap," in *The Review of English Studies*, vol. 1, pp. 72–74.

⁹ "The Suspected Revels Books," in *The Review of English Studies*, April, 1925, vol. 1, pp. 166–72.

¹⁰ As to this *cf.* Professor Albert Feuillerat's splendid work, *Documents Relating to the Office of the Revels in the Reign of Queen Elizabeth*, Louvain, 1908, especially pp. 450, 452, 456, and 461.

PAGE 5

¹¹ *A Life of William Shakespeare*, 6th ed., 1916, p. 649.

¹² 1923, vol. 4, p. 139.

¹³ *The Year's Work in English Studies*, 1927, p. 142.

CHAPTER II

PAGE 7

¹ Mr. Wood is in error here: erasures and alterations do occur in the Accounts.

² Mr. Wood was evidently of the opinion that there was no blotting paper in Shakspere's day. In this he was in error. *Cf.* the *New English Dictionary*.

PAGE 8

³ It must be noted that Professor Dobbie was not told that the document *as a whole* might be a recent forgery. He took it for granted that the other pages were "260 years old."

PAGE 9

⁴ Mr. Wood, we may recall, says that the alterations and erasures *are* in a different ink; and so they are. *Cf.* facsimile 3.

PAGE 10

⁵ It may, of course, be objected that I have not studied the originals and have made no chemical analysis of the ink. It is, however, fortunately true that, apart from the chemical analysis (which the British government would not permit me to make, in any case), the study of photographic enlargements of a questioned document not only is equal, but is even superior, to the study of the original. As to this the reader is referred to Chapter IV of Mr. Albert S. Osborn's *Questioned Documents*, Rochester, 1910.

CHAPTER III

PAGE 11

[1] This suggestion seems to have been first made by the late Horace Howard Furness, in his edition of *Othello*, p. 356.

[2] *Times Literary Supplement* (London), February 10, 1921, p. 91.

[3] In what follows I shall refer to the 1604-5 Book as A and the 1611-12 Book as B; in referring to the pages in these books I shall say "3A" when I mean the third page of the earlier Book, "8B" when I mean the eighth page of the later Book, and "3A16" when I mean the sixteenth line on page 3 of Book A, and so forth.

PAGE 12

[4] This utterly unwarranted statement is repeated by Sir Edmund K. Chambers (*The Elizabethan Stage*, vol. 4, p. 137) on the authority, undoubtedly, of Mr. Law. Sir Edmund has written me that he made no personal examination of the documents. The formal Gothic letters occurring in the play-list exactly duplicate the similarly "printed" Gothic letters in other parts of the Accounts. (*Cf.* facsimile 1*a*.)

[5] Honyng was appointed Clerk Controller of the Tents and Revels on October 15, 1584, resigned that office on June 21, 1596, and returned to the Office of the Revels in 1603. *Cf.* Albert Feuillerat, *op. cit.*, p. 438. I may mention that not a single one of the unquestioned Revels Accounts bears Honyng's signature.

[6] "Aleven" for "eleven" is not, strictly speaking, Jacobean. It occurs in the manuscript of the celebrated Addition to the play of *Sir Thomas Moore* (1593): "he that will not see a red hearing at a harry grote, butter at a levenpence a pounde . . . lyst to me." The *New English Dictionary* shows that the word "eleven" was frequently spelled with the initial *a* even in the latter half of the sixteenth century, and it records an instance of "aleven" as early as 1400.

[7] Is it conceivable that Mr. Law's "illiterate scribe" is identical with Sir Edward Thompson's "professional scribe"?

[8] The statement regarding the non-interpolation of any of these pages should not be accepted too readily. The identity of the watermarks in all the pages is not proof that the books are made up of original sheets. Experts know how to join sheets of paper in such a way as to deceive all but the most skilled examiners.

[9] Mr. Law reads, erroneously: "playes shold." My reading agrees with that of Professor Feuillerat, and is undoubtedly correct.

[10] *Cf.* A. Feuillerat, *op. cit.*, pp. 450, 472, etc. The Book of Accounts for 1587-89 is the last one to have survived from the Elizabethan period.

PAGE 13

[11] This document, dated October 18, 1564, was discovered by Cunningham and transcribed by him, with many inaccuracies, in his *Extracts*, p. xx. It is at the Public Record Office in London.

[12] A study of the penmanship of the privy seals of the years 1604 and 1605, written (I think) by Hugh Alington, has almost convinced me that the writer of the suspected documents was imitating either Alington's hand or, more probably, that of the clerk who wrote the 1587-88 accounts.

[13] Mr. Law, it is true, does not say that the writer of the latter play-list was an illiterate scribe; but if a person who writes "Octobar," "aleven," and "Shaxberd," may be so designated, then surely one who writes "Duck" for *Duke*, "Aiedg" for *Age*, "woere" for *were*, "Coque" for *Quoque*, "Ruing" for *Running*, may have the adjective "illiterate" applied to him.

[14] No; the bulk of the writing is in the Old English or "secretary" hand.

PAGE 14

[15] For a detailed account of these and other personal characteristics in penmanship the reader must consult Mr. Osborn's *Questioned Documents*.

[16] Cunningham omitted this and the succeeding items from his transcripts of the Revels Accounts. For an explanation of these (and other) omissions, see Appendix E.

[17] = £293, 14s. 4d.

CHAPTER IV

PAGE 16

[1] See the present writer's short but comprehensive essay on the spelling and pronunciation of the poet's surname by his contemporaries in *The Dial* (Chicago), May 11, 1916, vol. 60, pp. 456–58.

PAGE 19

[2] *The Elizabethan Stage*, vol. 4, p. 139.

[3] The omitted paragraph presents a noteworthy and perhaps unique peculiarity: it omits the name of the reigning monarch and therefore makes 1604 the second year of the "reign" of Edmund Tylney. This error and the contradiction implied in its "Sc̄do" are probably partially responsible for Cunningham's omission of the paragraph from his *Extracts*. *Cf.* Appendix E and facsimile 2.

PAGE 20

[4] Mr. Law is guilty of a serious error here. The paragraphs omitted by Cunningham assert that the Master had been paid £100 *in advance* for the ensuing year and that £66, 9s. 10d. were due him from the preceding year. See Appendix E.

[5] Professor Feuillerat has kindly written me that he intended to say no more than that in the Accounts he was editing he had discovered no evidence that Cunningham had tampered with the documents or made any fraudulent additions to them.

PAGE 21

[6] *Cf.* "Supposed Shakespeare Forgeries," by D. T. B. Wood, in TLS, July 2, 1924.

[7] The fact, too, that Cunningham's book abounds in fulsome praise of Collier cannot be without significance in this connection.

[8] *Cf. Life of Edmond Malone*, by Sir James Prior, 1860, p. 294.

[9] *Cf.* E. K. Chambers, *op. cit.*, vol. 4, p. 138.

PAGE 22

[10] Fleay's conjectural identification of this "lost" play with Heywood's *The Wise Woman of Hogsdon* has nothing to support it.

[11] In his edition of this play, in Dodsley's *Collection of Old Plays* (1825), Collier printed a dedicatory sonnet to Sir Thomas Walsingham. Recent investigation has shown that this sonnet exists only in a single copy of the play, is printed on an inserted leaf, and is undoubtedly a forgery. (*Cf.* T. J. Wise, *Athenæum*, 1908, vol. 1, pp. 788–89, and T. M. Parrott, *The Plays and Poems of George Chapman*, vol. 2, p. 726.)

[12] In fact, the paper shows three or four tiny holes at this point. (*Cf.* facsimile 13*b*.)

[13] "Was Peter Cunningham a Forger?" *Modern Language Review*, January, 1924, vol. 19, pp. 25–34.

PAGE 23

[14] *A Biographical Chronicle of the English Drama*, 1891, p. 96.

[15] Sir Edmund Chambers asserts (*op. cit.*, vol. 2, p. 244) that the Duke of York's Company "played at Court, as it would seem, *only before the younger members of the family*." If Sir Edmund is right, there is nothing to corroborate the 1612 play-list's statement that the play was performed by the Duke of York's Players, inasmuch as the Revels Accounts deal only with "Playes & Jnventions; as was presented, & sett forthe *before ye kinges Matie*."

[16] I am indebted to Sir Edmund Chambers, to whom I communicated my find, for the information that "A. J. K. was no doubt A. J. Kemp, the editor of the *Losely Papers*, who was employed in 1840 at the Record Office. . . . He was not a first rate antiquarian and may well have given the regnal year wrong. But I do not see [nor do I] how he came to say [as he did] that there were no names of patentees. The patent itself is on the Patent Roll for 8 Jac. I, part 8" (*Patent Roll 1846, item 19*). Collier may have looked up this patent and, for reasons of his own, refrained from publishing a correction of A. J. K.'s unaccountable misstatement. The license, I may add, is undoubtedly genuine.

[17] *Cf.* Mrs. Stopes, *The Seventeenth Century Accounts of the Master of the Revels*, 1922, p. 21; also her reply to Mr. Lawrence in *Modern Language Review*, July, 1924, p. 343.

PAGE 24

[18] *Elizabethan Stage*, vol. 3, p. 441.

[19] We must also consider the possibility that if two forgers were at work on these Accounts, the principal need not have taken his accessory into his whole confidence, or that he might have thought an occasional blunder, especially one which could be readily detected, a desideratum as tending to allay suspicion.

[20] The MS. really reads "The Morr of Veins", "Morr" being altered to "Moor." This is one of the entries in which something resembling a capital *J* was altered to a *T*.

[21] Mr. Lawrence does not specify the evidence on which he bases his assertion.

[22] In the journal of the Prince of Wirtemberg's visit to London in 1610 there is an entry, in French, that His Eminence visited the Globe and witnessed a performance of "l'histoire du More de Venise." We know from Sir H. Mildmay's manuscript diary that on May 6, 1635, he attended a performance of "a play Called the More of Venice."

PAGE 25

[23] For reasons which Chapter VIII will make apparent, I leave out of consideration the entry about "the moore of venice" in the questioned play-list of 1636–37.

PAGE 26

[24] That Malone made his memorandum on the flyleaf of his copy of *The Silver Age* near the close of his life, *i.e.*, when his eyesight was growing steadily worse, seems to me inferable from the fact that the penmanship is very much worse than that of the memoranda in his other books, viz., *The Changeling*, *Amyntas*, Baker's *Biographia Dramatica*, Langbaine's *Account of the English Dramatic Poets*, etc.

[25] This play-list does not give the names of the poets "which mayd the plaies." *Cf.* Appendix D, p. 69.

PAGE 27

[26] For a possible explanation of this puzzling item, *cf. A Life of William Shakespeare*, by Professor Joseph Q. Adams, 1923, pp. 371–72.

[27] *Seventeenth Century Accounts*, 1922.

PAGE 28

[28] *Cf.* Henry B. Wheatley's *Notes on the Life of John Payne Collier*, London, 1884, p. 56.

[29] *Cf. Notes and Queries*, May 5, 1906, pp. 347–48, communication by Professor T. M. Parrott.

[30] *Cf.* "Chapman's *All Fools* and J. P. Collier," by T. M. Parrott, *Athenæum*, London, June 27, 1908, pp. 788–89.

PAGE 29

[31] Professor Feuillerat has studied these two paragraphs with me and assures me that they are inexplicable. The only suggestion I can make is that the forger did not understand the true meaning of the Latin paragraph which he had transcribed from some genuine document or memorandum.

CHAPTER V

PAGE 31

[1] SSF, pp. 65–66.

PAGE 32

[2] One who is inclined to demand infallibility from an "expert," as is so often the case in courts of law, will probably not attach much value to Professor Wallace's opinion

as to the authenticity of these papers, and will point out that in his American lectures Professor Wallace declared certain spurious Shakspere autographs, in books belonging to the British Museum, genuine! For facsimiles of these "Shakspere autographs," *cf.* my book, *Problems in Shakspere's Penmanship*, New York, 1927.

PAGE 33

[3] *Cf. Henslowe's Diary*, edited by Walter W. Greg, 1904, vol. 1, p. xxxvj.

[4] *The Athenæum*, 1911, vol. 2, pp. 297, 324, 388; 1912, vol. 1, pp. 390, 470.

PAGE 35

[5] This ink is slightly more gray and less dark than the other ink (which shades from a blackish brown to a lighter brown). Examination of the document with the comparison or color microscope and with Lovibond tintometer glasses would undoubtedly yield interesting results. *Cf.* A. S. Osborn's *The Problem of Proof*, 1922, pp. 412–13, or *Questioned Documents*, pp. 355–62.

[6] Collier, we may recall, had the effrontery to charge the authorities of the British Museum with having tampered with his "Perkins Folio."

[7] *Extracts*, p. 211.

[8] The difference between these letters and the rest of the writing, in the *l*'s, the curved strokes, the tint of the ink, etc., is strikingly shown in a photographic facsimile.

PAGE 38

[9] In the numbering of these lines I have ignored the date at the top of the page.

PAGE 39

[10] For a full exposition of the subject of retouching, *cf.* Mr. Osborn's *Questioned Documents*, pp. 270–72, etc.

PAGE 40

[11] *Cf.* P. Fitzgerald, *A New History of the Stage*, 1882, vol. 1, p. 150.

PAGE 41

[12] In the absence of a model a forger is very apt to print a name, because he thinks that printing does not vary so much as writing. To my great regret none of my friends, not even Professor Feuillerat, could refer me to an unquestionably genuine Honyng signature.

PAGE 42

[13] Sotherton's Old English signature, as we see it in *MS. Lansd. 83,f. 171* (January 5, 1597), is very different from his Roman signature. (*Cf.* facsimiles 4*b* and 8.)

CHAPTER VI

PAGE 43

[1] *Memoranda on 'Measure for Measure,'* London, 1880, pp. 9–10.

[2] In a note to a passage in Dryden's *Grounds of Criticism*, ed. 1800, pp. 258–59, Malone says: "I formerly thought

that *Othello* was one of our great dramatic poet's latest compositions, but I now *know, from indisputable evidence*, that was not the case." Unfortunately, Malone did not mention the source of his knowledge. Those who are acquainted with the history of the Alleyn manuscripts know, of course, that a number of documents studied and transcribed by Malone are now lost. Whether he failed to return them, or whether they disappeared after he returned them and before Collier studied the Dulwich collection, it is impossible to say.

[3] J. O. Halliwell-Phillipps, *Outlines of the Life of Shakespeare*, 1885, p. 607.

[4] *A New Variorum: Othello*, p. 356. Dr. Furness was not at all convinced by Halliwell-Phillipps's argument.

[5] Cope's letter was published in 1872 (in the *Third Report of the Royal Commission of Historical Manuscripts*) and is facsimiled and transcribed in Ingleby's *Centurie of Prayse*, 1874, pp. 11, 45. Mrs. Stopes, however, points out that the Cecil Papers, the Cope letter among them, were well known to scholars before 1872, "as Secretaries superintended the Library at Hatfield and students were admitted to study the reigns of Elizabeth and James."

[6] *A New Variorum: The Tempest*, p. 280, footnote. In my quotation from Furness I have emphasized the word "entire" because Mr. Law omitted it altogether.

PAGE 44

[7] This letter (*cf.* facsimile 11), at first erroneously addressed to "Anthony Malone," is now at the Bodleian Library and is by some supposed to refer to the "scrap," although the wording of the note makes that almost impossible. Sir William would undoubtedly have made a point of the fact that the newly discovered document was a Revels Book of Accounts, if it had been that.

[8] *Cf.* his letter, "Supposed Shakespeare Forgeries," in *The Times Literary Supplement*, July 2, 1924.

[9] *Cf.* his essay, "The Revels Books: the Writer of the Malone Scrap," in *The Review of English Studies*, January, 1925, vol. 1, pp. 72–74.

PAGE 45

[10] We must not lose sight of the fact that the "scrap" epitomizes only the 1604–5 play-list.

[11] *The Elizabethan Stage*, vol. 4, pp. 137–38.

PAGE 46

[12] Boswell's Malone, 1821, vol. 2, p. 463.

[13] *Extracts*, p. 225.

[14] *Cf. A Supplemental Apology*, 1799, pp. 342–43, 404, 413. Chalmers was of the opinion that both *Henry V* and *Measure for Measure* contained flattering delineations of King James. Would it be unfair to suggest that the forger included these two plays in his play-list because he approved of Chalmers's opinion regarding them?

PAGE 47

[15] *More about Shakespeare 'Forgeries,'* pp. 59–60.

[16] Mr. Wood informs us ("The Suspected Revels Books," in *The Review of English Studies*, April, 1925, p. 166) that Sir William Musgrave, sixth Bart., was Commissioner of

Customs from 1763 to 1785, Commissioner for Auditing Public Accounts from 1785 till his death in 1800, became a Fellow of the Society of Antiquaries in 1774 (and a Vice President in 1786), and was from 1783 a Trustee of the British Museum.

¹⁷ "The Revels Books," p. 73.

PAGE 48

¹⁸ Mr. Wood evidently meant to say that the paper of the "scrap" is identical with that which Collier employed in some of his correspondence in 1839.

PAGE 50

¹⁹ This will appear from a study of facsimiles of the hand-writing of Malone, Steevens, Collier, and many of their contemporaries, in books dealing with autographs, and in the catalogues of booksellers. I found many of these characteristics recently in a study of Washington Irving's penmanship. And we may quote Mr. Wood himself ("The Revels Books," p. 2) to the effect that the British Museum "contains a number of letters of Payne Collier [!] in a hand not very dissimilar to that of the Malone Scrap."

²⁰ In studying Musgrave's handwriting I have had before me photostats of his letter to Malone (*Bodl., Malone MS. 27, f. 15,* dated December 2, 1799), the two-page letter facsimiled by Mr. Wood (*B.M., Add. MSS. 34420, f. 24,* dated June 7, 1785), penciled memoranda in *Add. MSS. 5750–56* (referred to by Mr. Wood), and a letter, dated February 3, 1796, from Musgrave to Malone, which is now the property of Dr. Horace H. Furness, Jr., and is referred to in the *New Variorum: Othello,* on p. 356. Of Collier's handwriting I have before me photostats of a page of his unpublished *History of the Restoration Stage*; of some four hundred and fifty pages of his unpublished manuscript work, *Emendations and Notes to Old Printed Plays*; of the scribbled inside of the annotated back cover of the "Perkins Folio" (now in the H. E. Huntington Library and Art Gallery); and of some of his letters.

PAGE 52

²¹ Collier's manuscript *History of the Restoration Stage* shows just such margins as we have in the "scrap."

CHAPTER VII

PAGE 54

¹ Mr. Law erroneously recognized (SSF, p. 64) only two styles of handwriting: Gothic, or Old English, and the Italian character.

PAGE 56

² There are many puzzling things about some of Collier's forgeries, but none perhaps is more puzzling than his statement (*loc. cit.*)—a statement which he must have known to be false—that "A comparison with this specimen of the penmanship of the Master of the Revels leaves no doubt that the inscription on an existing copy of the play of *Locrine,* 4to 1595, assigning the authorship of it to Charles Tylney, is the handwriting of Sir George Buck." A more impudent prevarication than this can hardly be

imagined. The inscription in *The Lamentable Tragedie of Locrine* (which I have been permitted to examine by the kindness of its present owner, Dr. A. S. W. Rosenbach) is written in imitation Old English "secretary"—I need hardly say it is a gross and palpable forgery—and bears not the remotest resemblance to the *Daphnis* inscription. Inasmuch as the *Locrine* inscription has never been read correctly, even by the late Dr. Graves, I transcribe it herewith: "Char. Tilney wrot[e]/Tragedy of this matter/ he named Estrild:/I think is this. it was l [?]/ by his death. A[?] w u[?]/fellon hath published/ I made dūbe shewes for it./wch I yet haue. G.B./" Hitherto this has been read thus: "Char. Tilney wrote *a* Tragedy of this matter *which* he named Estrild: *which* I think is this. it was *lost* by his death. *A wise fellow* hath published it. I made dumbe showes for it *when I it saw.* G.B." My italics indicate inexcusable errors and additions. (*Cf.* facsimile 14*c.*)

PAGE 57

³ For an instructive paper on this subject, see Professor Hazelton Spencer's essay, "The Forger at Work: a New Case against Collier," in *The Philological Quarterly,* January, 1927, vol. 6, pp. 32–38.

CHAPTER VIII

PAGE 58

¹ MASF, p. 36.

PAGE 59

² For such a study as this the reader must have access to an enlarged photograph or photostat of the original. A reduced facsimile, especially a half-tone, such as that furnished by Mr. Law in his second book, at p. 39, is worthless in the study of a questioned document.

³ Malone's transcript of Herbert's now lost Book of Accounts records only fourteen performances. (*Cf.* Malone's *Historical Account of the Rise and Progress of the English Stage,* Basil, 1800, pp. 299–300.) In the forged 1636–37 play-list, recording twenty-two performances, two of the plays not mentioned by Malone are "the moore of venice" and "hamlett." It is at least curious that material under suspicion so often contains data of Shaksperian interest.

PAGE 60

⁴ A transcript of the document, which purports to be a bill presented by the Blackfriars Company for Court performances in the year 1637, is given on p. 404 of Professor Adams's book.

PAGE 61

⁵ *Cf. The Journal of the British Archaeological Association,* December, 1860, p. 344.

⁶ It may be noticed that "1792" is one of the numbers in the upper right corner of the document. Someone had evidently been computing the age of the document.

PAGE 62

⁷ In an interesting little book, *Archaeologic and Historic Fragments. Containing, inter alia, a facsimile of a rare MS. page dated 1638, having reference to two of Shakespeare's*

most famous plays, with notes thereon (London, 1887, pp. 1–15), Mr. Wright supplies the following additional information: "The original page, or, rather, leaflet, by mere accident, came into my hands whilst looking through the dramatic collection of my old friend, the late Mr. Drinkwater Meadows, the famous comedian, of now more than thirty years ago." In a footnote (on p. 2) he adds: "This curious and unique page of writing was sold after the lamented death of its owner, with his books and other MSS., by Messrs. Puttick and Simpson, and fetched the large sum of five pounds, as was told me by Mrs. Drinkwater Meadows." I think it not unworthy of mention that Mr. Wright, in this much expanded version of his original essay on this play-list, says not a word about Isaac Reed, the *Notitia Dramatica*, the memorandum on the back of the sheet, or the late Sir W. Fordyce. What we are to infer from all this, let the reader judge.

APPENDIX A

PAGE 63

[1] So untrained for his task was Sir James that he did not know that the examination of a questioned document "while you wait" is, as a rule, of negligible value.

[2] Professor Dobbie errs here. The suspicion was, of course, that the play-lists were fabricated shortly before the date of their publication (1842). Sir James was not sufficiently informed regarding the question at issue.

PAGE 64

[3] Professor Dobbie, be it remembered, did not examine the signatures chemically.

APPENDIX B

PAGE 65

[1] For an account of this manuscript, see *The Tempest* (ed. H. H. Furness), p. 275.

[2] Warrant.

[3] Marston's *Dutch Courtesan* (1603–4).

[4] A lost play.

[5] Letters.

[6] These words occur in the left margin.

[7] Fletcher and Shakspere's lost [?] *History of Cardenio* (see E. H. C. Oliphant, *The Plays of Beaumont and Fletcher*, 1927, pp. 286–90).

PAGE 66

[8] A lost play.

[9] A lost play by Richard Niccolls.

[10] A lost play by Cyril Tourneur.

[11] This may be the play of *Caesar's Revenge* which was published anonymously in 1607 (see E. K. Chambers, *The Elizabethan Stage*, vol. 4, p. 4).

[12] This is probably a John Ford play.

[13] By Fletcher [?].

[14] Shakspere's *I Henry IV*.

[15] Shakspere's *Much Ado about Nothing*.

[16] These words ('get the Council's warrant') are in the left margin.

[17] By Beaumont and Fletcher.

[18] By George Chapman.

APPENDIX C

PAGE 67

[1] "1604" was clumsily altered to "1605."

[2] The word "names" was deleted with four horizontal strokes.

[3] This word was altered to "Moor."

[4] "Jons" was clumsily altered to "Jhons."

[5] A ghostly *e* appears after "mor."

PAGE 68

[6] The last two letters were crowded into the line and are not identifiable.

[7] The last three letters are not identifiable.

[8] A ghostly *e* appears after "on."

[9] A ghostly *ye* appears after the *d* in "Tragide."

[10] This is the spot where several tiny holes appear in the paper.

APPENDIX D

PAGE 69

[1] The last three letters look as if they had been written on damp paper.

[2] The last five letters look as if they had been written on damp paper.

[3] After the *d* there is the upper half of an *e*.

[4] "On . . . Ring," one line in the manuscript.

[5] "Nobelmen" altered to "Nobilmen."

[6] "Twelfe . . . Hid," one line in the manuscript.

[7] "price" altered to "prize."

[8] An error for "Prince."

[9] "St" was clumsily altered to "Sh."

[10] "Haliday" changed to "Holiday," or the reverse.

NOTES ON FACSIMILES

FACSIMILE 1 (p. 15).—These are the author's free imitations (not exact duplicates) of certain letters occurring in Books A and B and in a document signed "Honynges."

FACSIMILE 2 (p. 83).—Note the close similarity between this and facsimile 19. It is transcribed, with many inaccuracies and two notable omissions, on p. 203 of Cunningham's *Extracts from the Accounts of the Revels at Court.*

FACSIMILE 3 (p. 84).—This is transcribed in Appendix C, p. 67. All previous transcripts contain many errors—a statement which applies also to facsimile 4*a*.

FACSIMILE 4*a* (p. 85).—The "ghosts" in the words "one" and "Spainshe" are considerably darker than in the manuscript.

FACSIMILE 4*b* (p. 85).—This is transcribed on p. 418 of Professor Feuillerat's *Documents Relating to the Office of the Revels.*

FACSIMILE 5 (p. 86).—This document is transcribed, with some inaccuracies, on p. xx of Cunningham's *Extracts.*

FACSIMILE 6 (p. 87).—For a transcript of this significant document, see p. 69. Because of typographic considerations, it was not practicable to make an exact type-facsimile of this page.

FACSIMILE 9 (p. 89).—For a transcript of this document, see Feuillerat's *Documents*, p. 379.

FACSIMILE 13a (p. 93).—This shows tampering as well as traces of Collier's penmanship.

FACSIMILE 13b (p. 93).—Note the watermark in the facsimile. A transmitted-light photograph shows erasures, retouching, and holes in the paper, as well as the writing on both sides of the sheet.

FACSIMILE 14c (p. 94).—The inscription, first brought to light by Collier, is not in Sir George Buc's handwriting. It is undoubtedly a forgery. Note that the words "which I yet have" are an after-addition and that the penultimate line was adapted to the letters "G. B."

FACSIMILE 17 (p. 97).—A transcript of this warrant, with a considerable number of errors, occurs on p. 71 of Mr. Law's *More about Shakespeare Forgeries*.

FACSIMILE 19 (p. 99).—This is transcribed, with the usual allotment of errors, on p. 210 of Cunningham's *Extracts*.

FACSIMILE 20 (p. 100).—This is transcribed, with errors, on pp. 213–14 of Cunningham's *Extracts*.

FACSIMILE 21 (p. 101).—For a transcript of this, see p. 209 of Cunningham's *Extracts*.

FACSIMILE 22 (p. 102).—This is transcribed by Professor Feuillerat, with his usual accuracy, in his book, *op. cit.*, p. 378. Note the marginal admonition: "the names of the plays wold [*sic*] be expressed."

FACSIMILES

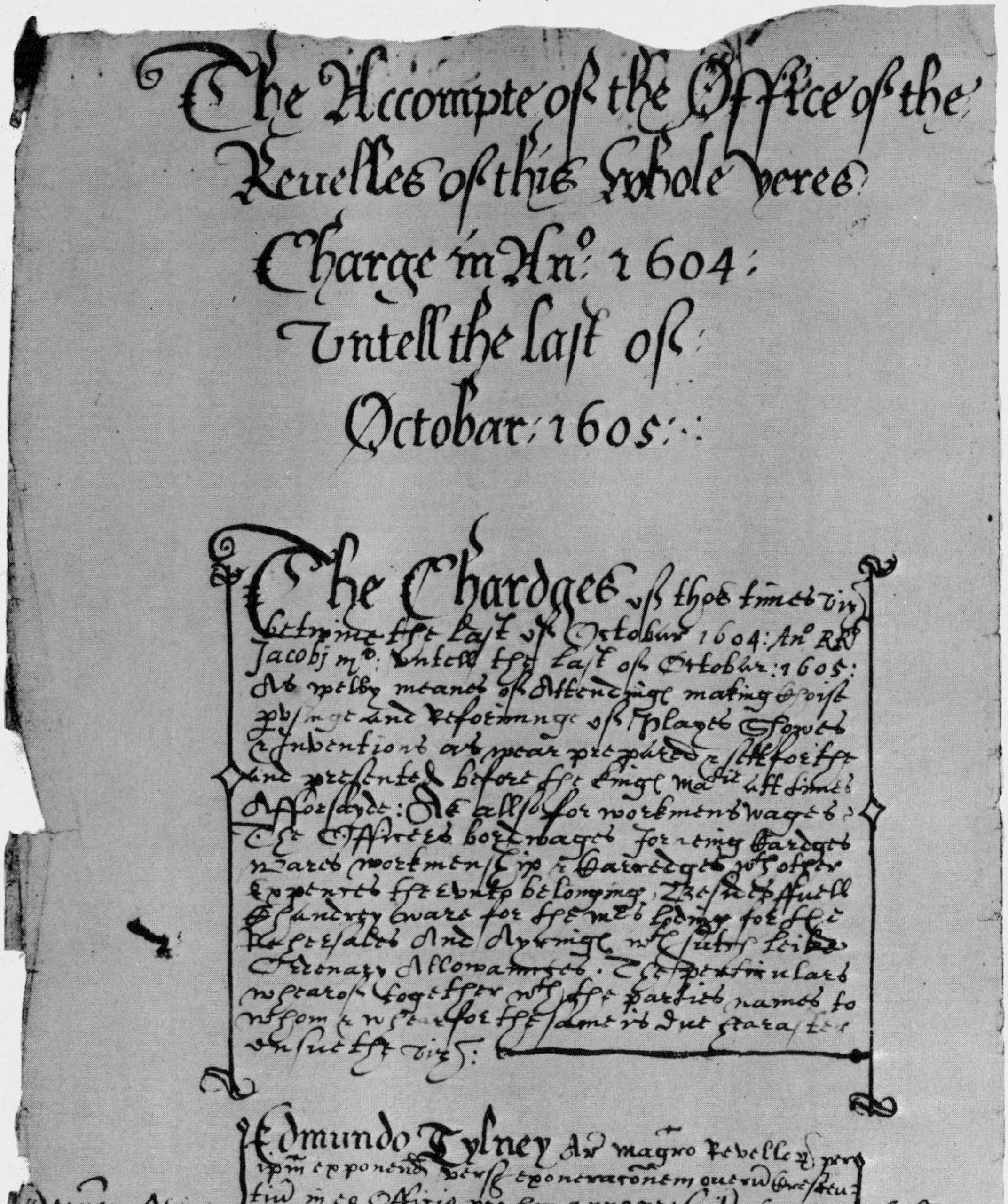

The Accompte of the Office of the
Reuelles of this whole yeres
Charge in An° 1604:
Untell the last of:
Octobar: 1605:

The Chardges of the tyme viz

[manuscript text in secretary hand — largely illegible]

Edmundo Tylney Ar magro Reuelles &c ...

[manuscript text in secretary hand — largely illegible]

FACSIMILE 2

SECOND PAGE OF BOOK A (1604-5)—*slightly reduced*

FACSIMILE 3

PLAY-LIST A, PAGE 3 OF BOOK A (1604-5)—*slightly reduced*

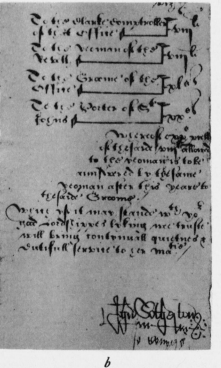

By his Ma^tis plaiers:: On Candelmas night A playe Every one Inhis umor

The Sunday ffollowing A playe prouided And disscharged

By his Ma^tis plaiers: On Shrousunday A play off the Marthant of venis Shaxberd

By his Ma^tis plaiers:. On Shroumonday A Tragidye of the Spanishe Mazj:

By his ma^tis players:- On Shroutusday A play Cauled Shaxberd The Martchant of venis Againe Comanded

a

c

b

d

FACSIMILE 4

a. LOWER PART OF PAGE 4 A   *b.* THE ENGROSSING CLERK'S HAND

c. WRITING, PROBABLY GENUINE, IN BOOK B   *d.* TITLE OF BOOK B

FACSIMILE 5

THE PRESTON WARRANT—*slightly reduced*

The names, of the playes And by what Cumphney [players] playde
them heareafter ffollowetg: And Allso what masked, and Triumph[?]
att the Tilte were presented before the kinge wtin this yeare 1611[?]

By the Kings players: Hallomas: Nyggt was presented att whitgall before ye kinge[?]
A play Called the Tempest:

The Kings players: The 5:th of nouember: A play Called ye winters nigts Tayley

The Kings players: On St Stiuenes night A play called Kinge no kinge [ruing at ye kin?]

The Queens players: St John: night A play Called the City Gallant.

The princes players: The sunday, ffollowinge A play called the Almanak

The Kings players: On neweres, night A play Called the Twins Tragedie
And ruing att the king[?]

The childern of whitfriers the Sunday ffollowing A play Called Cupids Reuenge
This day the Kings prince, Twelfe, night the princes Mask performed by Gentelmen of his[?]
wth diuer of his Noblemen
did run att ye Rina for
a prize.

By the Queens players The sunday, ffollowinge att Grinwidg before the Queen And
and the Kings men the prince was playd the Siluer Aidg: And ye next night following Lucrie[?]

By the Queens players Candelmas: night A play Called Tu Coque

By the Kings players Shroue sunday: A play Called the Noblman

By the Duck of yorks Shroue: Munday: A play Called Hmens Haliday
players /

By the Laydy: Elizabeths Shroue: Teuesday A play Called the proud Mayds Tragedie
players /

On the: 24: day of marche Being the Kings Ma:tis day
of his Entrie to the Croune of England was performed at ye
Tilt A Triumphs for.

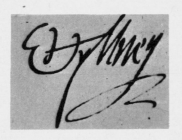

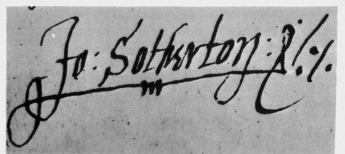

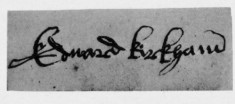

FACSIMILE 7

SIGNATURES AND WRITING ON PAGE 7A—*slightly enlarged*

FACSIMILE 8

GENUINE SIGNATURES—*some enlarged*

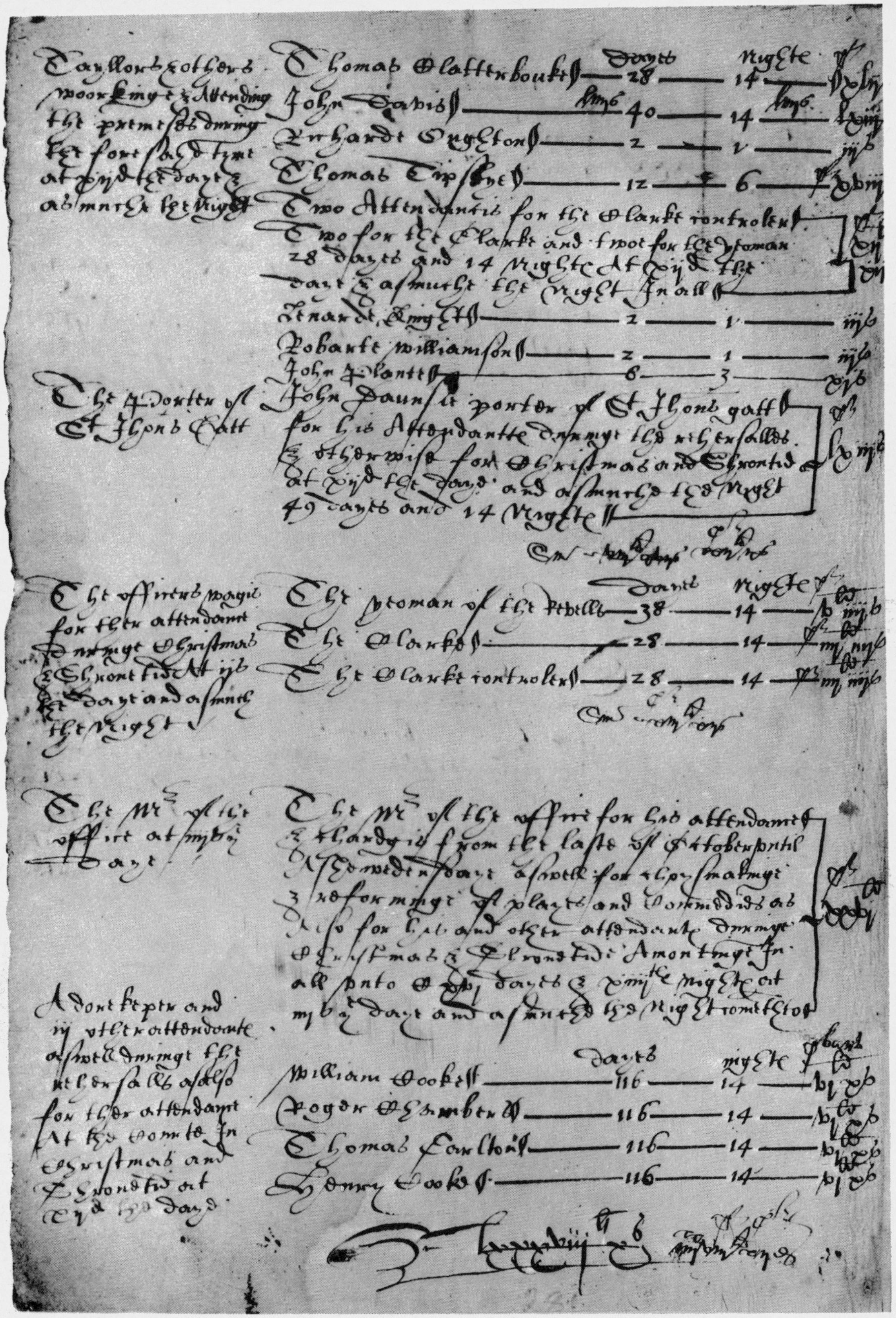

Taylors & others working & attending the premisses during the foresaid time at xijd the daye & asmuche the night

		Dayes	Nightes
	Thomas Clatterbooke	28	14
	John Davies	40	14
	Richarde Singleton	2	1
	Thomas Tipsley	12	6
	Two Attendantes for the Clarke controller Two for the Clarke and two for the yoman 28 dayes and 14 nightes at xijd the daye & asmuche the night in all		
	Richarde Knight	2	1
	Robarte Williamson	2	1
	John Plantt	8	3

The Porter of St Johns Gate — John Dauncer porter of St Johns gate for his attendaunce during the rehersalles & otherwise for Christmas and Shrovetide at xijd the daye and asmuche the night 49 dayes and 14 nightes

The officers wage for their attendance during Christmas & Shrovetide at ijs the daye and asmuch the night

	Dayes	Nightes
The yoman of the Revelles	38	14
The Clarke	28	14
The Clarke controller	28	14

The Mr of the office — The Mr of the office for his attendance & chardges from the laste of October untill Ashwednesdaye aswell for the perusinge & reforminge of playes and Commedies as also for his and other attendance during Christmas & Shrovetide amountinge in all unto cxvj dayes & xiiij nightes

A porter kepte and iij other attendauntes aswell during the rehersalles as also for their attendance at the Courte in Christmas and Shrovetide at xijd the daye

	Dayes	Nightes
William Bookell	116	14
Roger Chamber	116	14
Thomas Carlton	116	14
Henry Cooke	116	14

FACSIMILE 9

PAGE 3 OF ACCOUNTS OF 1587-88

1604 & 1605   Ed.ᵈ Tylney

Sunday after Hallowmas ___ Merry wiues of
    Windsor perf.ᵈ by the Kᵍˢ players

Hallamas ___ in the Banquettingho.ᵘ at Whitehall
    the Moor of Venis ___ perf.ᵈ by the Kᵍˢ players

On S.ᵗ Stephens night ___ Mesure for Mesur
    by Shaxberd ___ perf.ᵈ by the Kᵍˢ players

on Innocents night Errон by Shaxberd
    perf.ᵈ by the Kᵍˢ players

on Sunday following " How to learne of a
    woman to wooe " by Hewood ___
    perf.ᵈ by the Q.ˢ players

on New years night ___ All fooles by G. Chapman
    perf.ᵈ by the Boyes of the Chapel

bet New y.ˢ day & twelfth day ___
    Loues Labour lost perf.ᵈ by the Kᵍˢ p.ⁿ

on the 7.ᵗʰ Ian. the Hen. the fifth perf.ᵈ by.ᵗʰ Kᵍˢ

on 8.ᵗʰ Ian ___ Every one out of his humour

on Candlemas night Every one in his humour

on Shrove sunday " the Marchant of Venis "
    by Shaxberd ___ perf.ᵈ by the Kᵍˢ P.ⁿ
___ the same repeated on Shrove tuesd. by the Kᵍˢ Comм

FACSIMILE 10

THE MALONE "SCRAP"

Park Place S.ᵗ James's
13. Feb: 96

Dear Sir

I certainly have not any objection
against your saying "that you have been informed that
"the original is still extant" and I think my friend cannot
consider it as any disobedience to the prohibition which
enjoins me not to betray the name of the person who is
in possession of that original.

In Camden's Annals of K. James I. — printed in the
2.ᵈ Vol. of the Collection of Historians" pa. 656 — under the
date of 14. Mar. 1621 — you will find the authority for the
quarrel between the M.ˢ of Bucks and [struck] the E. of Southampton
It is in these words " There was some quarelling between the
"M.ˢ of B. and Southampton & Sheffield who had interrupted
"him, for repeating the same thing over and over again, and
"that contrary to the received approved Order in Parliament; but
"the Prince reconciled them"

I have 5 Autographs of Q. Eliz. 2. in the 1.ˢᵗ y.ʳ of
her reign & one in the 5.ᵗʰ 10.ᵗʰ & 15.ᵗʰ years respectively
Yours most truly —   W. Musgrave

FACSIMILE II

LETTER FROM MUSGRAVE TO MALONE

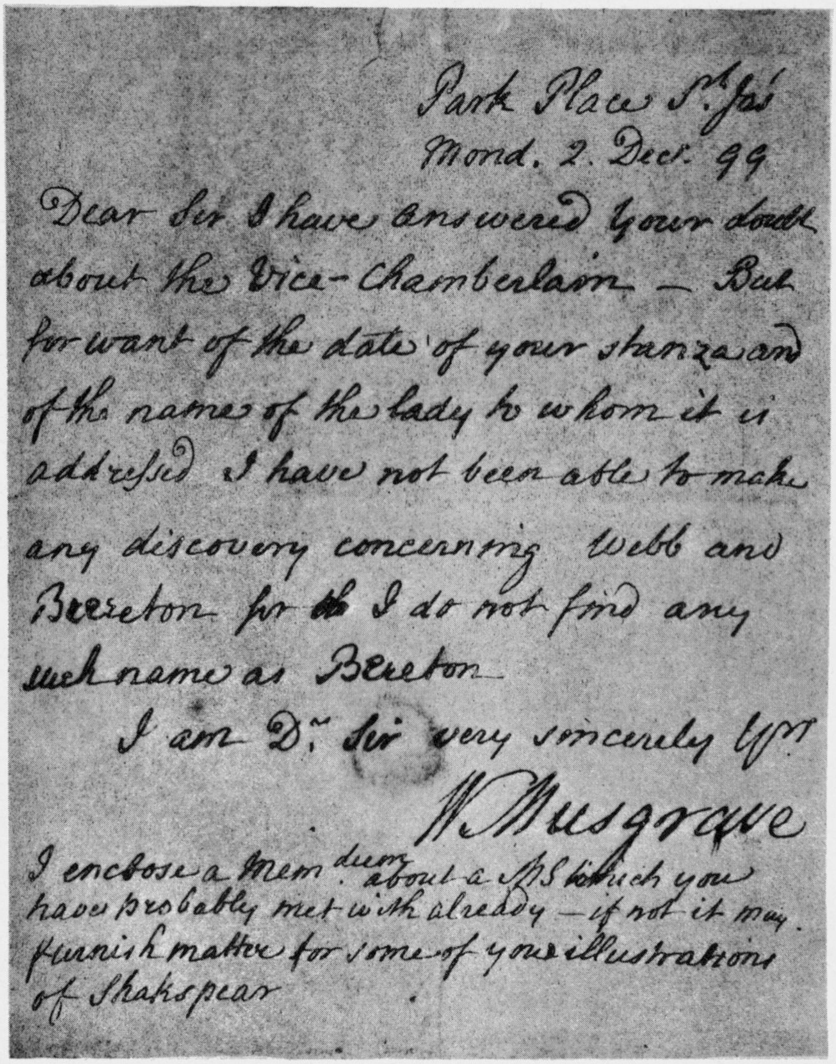

Park Place St. Jas
Mond. 2. Dec. 99

Dear Sir I have answered your doubt about the Vice-Chamberlain — But for want of the date of your stanza and of the name of the lady to whom it is addressed I have not been able to make any discovery concerning Webb and Brereton for I do not find any such name as Brereton

I am Dr. Sir very sincerely Yrs

W Musgrave

I enclose a Memdum. about a MS which you have probably met with already — if not it may furnish matter for some of your illustrations of Shakspear

FACSIMILE 12

LETTER FROM MUSGRAVE TO MALONE

FACSIMILE 13

a. PART OF THE LEFT MARGIN OF PLAY-LIST B—*enlarged*

b. PART OF PAGES 3A AND 4A—*seen by transmitted light*

a

b

c

FACSIMILE 14

a. A PAGE OF COLLIER'S UNPUBLISHED *Emendations*

b. A FORGED INSCRIPTION IN BUC'S *Daphnis Polustephanos*

c. A FORGED INSCRIPTION IN A *Locrine* QUARTO (1595)

Two Noble Kinsmen A I s 1 (Dyce XI, 338)

Wars or "war"

The old editions read thus, in the speech of Theseus, ~~[crossed out]~~ referring to her marriage:—
"This is a service, whereto I am going, Greater than any war"

Theobald corrected "war" to wars, but he ought to have made it wars — in the plural, which not only was the usual word of the time, as innumerable instances would establish, but must have been the word of the poet. Either the letter s accidentally dropped out in the press,

a

The warrant for paym.t of 240.li vnto End Knight yp Players for yp playe Nooke

1636) 1637

1631 d 1637

v.to July 34

Rec.d in p.te of t vng ...

b

Dido 2. of Carth. A IV. (Dyce II. 416)

Coil or "coll"

A very pretty figure of speech, and a clumsy expression substituted, by the wrong use of a single letter in a word in the soliloquy of Æneas, where he is anticipating how Dido would treat him, if he stayed to take leave of her: he ought to

a

c

FACSIMILE 15

a. TWO FRAGMENTS FROM COLLIER'S *Emendations*

b. ENDORSEMENT ON THE BACK OF THE PEMBROKE WARRANT

c. WRITING, PROBABLY GENUINE, ON TITLE-PAGE OF BOOK B

(22)   Playes acted before the kinge and Queene
this present yeare of the lord. 1636.

1 Easter munday at the Cockpitt the first parte of Arbiragus
2 Easter tuesday at the Cockpitt the second parte of Arbiragus
3 The 21 of Aprill at the Cockpitt the silent woman.
4 The 5. of may at the Blackfryers for the Queenes   Alfonso
   and the prince Elector ——————————————————

5 The 17th of November at hampton Courte. the Doprombe.
6 The 19th of November at hampton Court. Craggis Bush.
7 The 29 of November at hampton Court. the maides tragedie
8 The 6th of December at hampton Court. the loyall subiect.
9 The 8. of December at hampton Court. the moore of venice
10 The 16th of December at hampton Court. Loues pilgrimage
11 the S. Stephens day at hampton Court. the first pte of Arbiragus
12 S. Johns Day at hampton Court. the second parte of Arbiragus.
13 The first day of January at hampton Court. loue and honor
14 The 5th of January at hampton Court. the Elder brother.
15 The 10 of January at hampton Court. the kinge & noe king.
16 The 12th of January the new play from Oxford the Royall slaue
17 The 17th of January at hampton Court —— Rollo.
18 The 24. of January at hampton Court —— hamlett.

19 The 31 of January at St. James. the tragedie of Cesar
20 The 9th of February at St. James. the wife for a month
21 The 16th of February at St. James. the Gouernour
22 The 21. of February at St. James. Aglaura.

                                              22: playes

FACSIMILE 16
THE PLAY-LIST OF 1636-37

Whereas by virtue of his Ma.ts Letters Patents bearing date the 16th of June 1625 made & granted in confirmation of divers Warrants & privy Seals unto you formerly directed in the time of o.r late Soueraigne Lord King James, you are (amongst other things) to make payment for Playes Acted before his Ma.tie: These are to pray and require you out of his Ma.ts Treasure in your charge to pay or cause to bee payde vnto John Lowen and Ioseph Taylor or either of them for themselues & the rest of the Company of his Ma.ts Players the summ: of Twohundred & Tenne poundes (being after the vsuall & accustomed rate of Tenne poundes for each play) for One and Twenty Playes by them Acted before his Ma.tie at Hampton Court & else where w.thin the space of a yeere ended in February last And that you likewise pay vnto them the summ: of thirtye poundes more for their paynes in studying & acting the new Play sent from Oxford called the royall Slaue which in all amounteth to the summ of Two hundred & forty poundes: And these together w.th their acquittance for the receipt thereof shall bee your warr.t Whitehall the 12.th of March 1636.

To .... William Vuedale k.nt Treã.r of his Ma.ts Chamber.

d: Iuny 1638

Rec.d the same day & yeare of S.r W.m Vuedale k.nt Trẽr of his Ma. Chamb.r the som.e of ....

Eylleardt Swanston

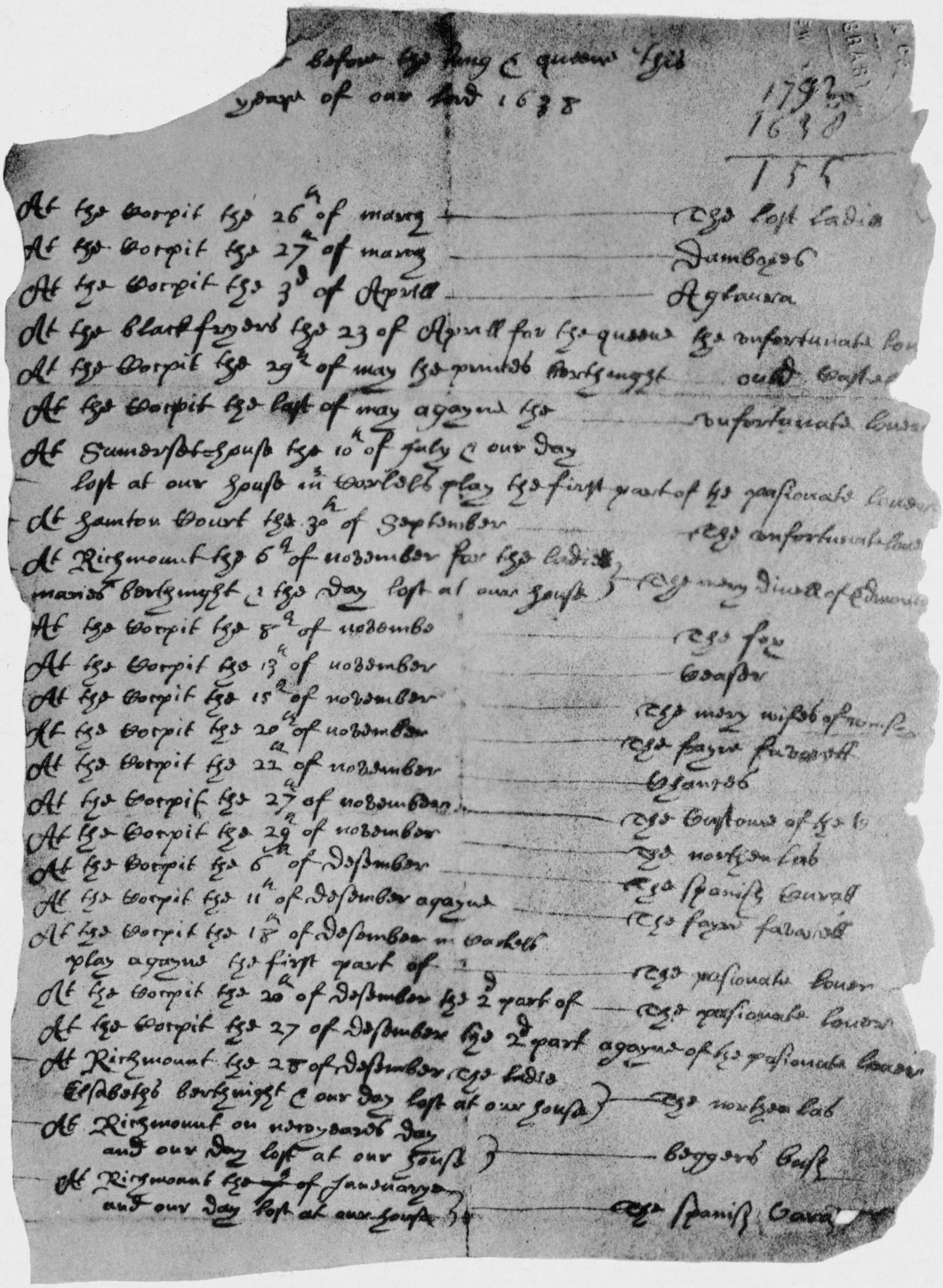

… before the king & queene this
yeare of our lord 1638

1792
1638
155

At the Cockpit the 26th of march — the lost ladie
At the Cockpit the 27th of march — Damboyes
At the Cockpit the 3d of Aprill — Aglaura
At the blackfryers the 23 of Aprill for the queene — the unfortunate lo[uers]
At the Cockpit the 29th of may the princes berthnyght — ould Castell
At the Cockpit the last of may agayne the — unfortunate louers
At Sumersethouse the 10th of July & our day
lost at our house in Carlels play the first part of the pasionate louers
At Hamton Court the 30th of September — the unfortunate louers
At Richmount the 6th of nouember for the ladie
maries berthnyght & the day lost at our house — the mery diuell of Edmonton
At the Cockpit the 8th of nouembr — the fox
At the Cockpit the 13th of nouember — Caesar
At the Cockpit the 15th of nouember — the mery wiues of winsor
At the Cockpit the 20th of nouember — the fayre favorett
At the Cockpit the 22th of nouember — Chances
At the Cockpit the 27th of nouember — the Costome of the c…
At the Cockpit the 29th of nouember — the northen lass
At the Cockpit the 6th of desember — the spanish curatt
At the Cockpit the 11th of desember agayne — the fayre favorett
At the Cockpit the 18th of desember in Carlels
play agayne the first part of — the pasionate louer
At the Cockpit the 20th of desember the 2 part of — the pasionate louers
At the Cockpit the 27 of desember the 2d part agayne of the pasionate louers
At Richmount the 28 of desember the ladie
Elsabeths berthnyght & our day lost at our house — the northen lass
At Richmount on neweyeares day
and our day lost at our house — beggers bush
At Richmount the 6 of Januarye
and our day lost at our house — the spanish Cura[t]

FACSIMILE 18

GEORGE WRIGHT'S PLAY-LIST OF 1638-39

The Chardges, of those tymes viz:
Betwene the last of October. 1611. Anni,
Reg: Regis Jacobj nono untell the first of
November. 1612. As welby meanes of the
Attendinge, makinge Choyse, devysing, and
Reformynge of plaeyes & Inventions, w^ch
was presented & sett forth, before ye kinge
M^tie: In tymes afforesayd: As allso for work-
mens wages, The Officers Bordwages,
wares, workmans hyer, Carredges, and
other Expences, thereto belonginge. As fuell,
and Chandrie ware, for the masters: & for
the Office, for rehearsalls, and Ayring, of
Stufe and Garments, wth suche leike ord-
narie Allowaunces, As hath bin Acoustomed,
heartofore Allowed. The p^ticuler,
whearofe, with the p^ties names to whome,
And wherfore, y^e same is dewe: unto
heareafter foloweth.

FACSIMILE 19

PART OF PAGE 2 OF BOOK B (1611-12)—*enlarged*

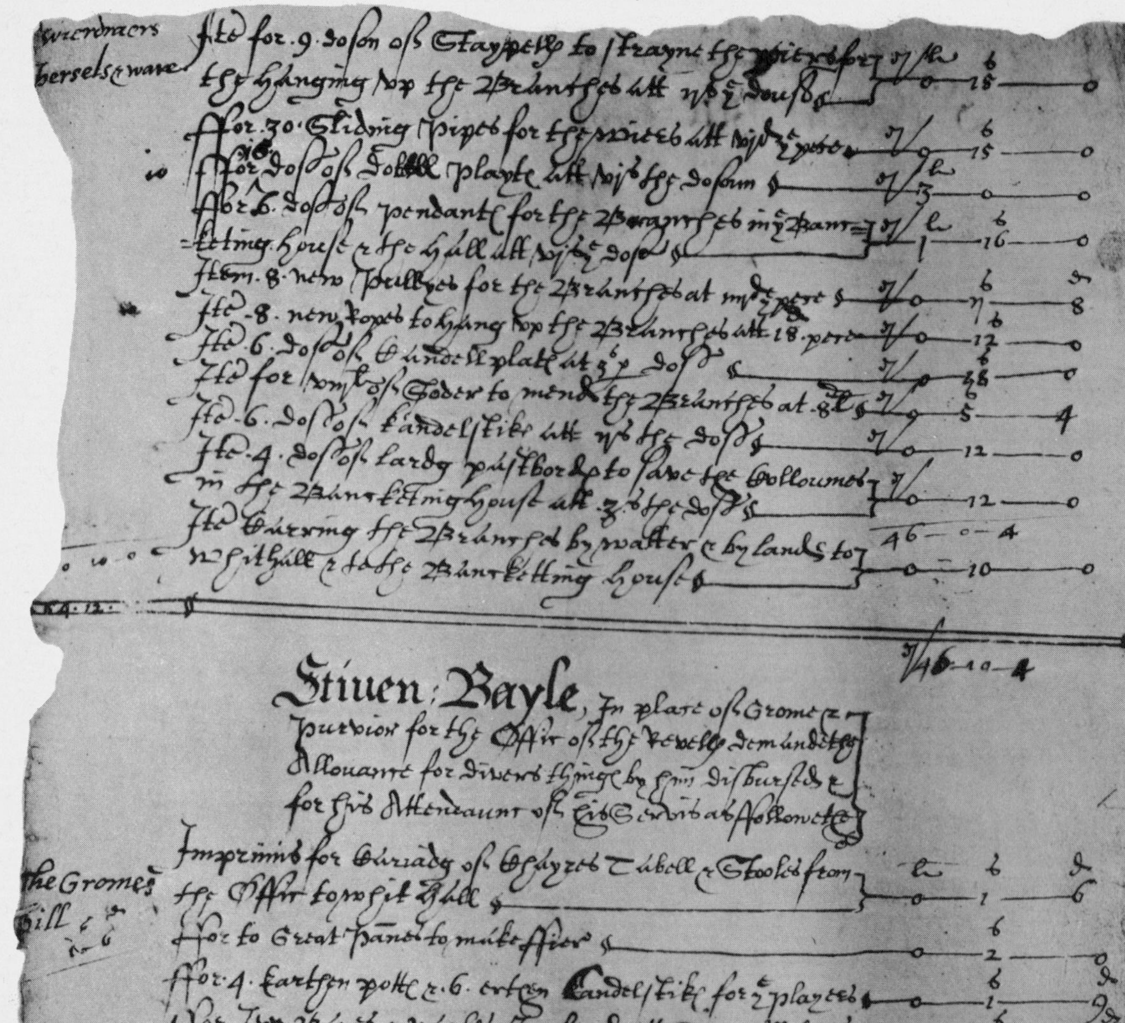

Stiuen Bayle

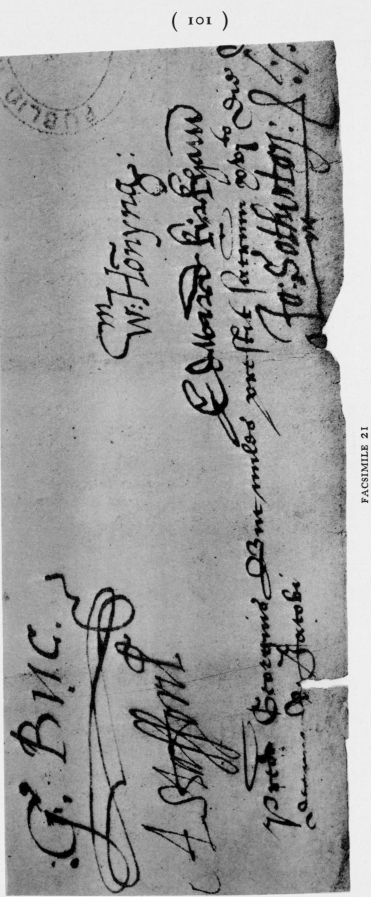

FACSIMILE 21

LOWER PART OF PAGE 7 OF BOOK B—*enlarged*

280

INDEX

INDEX